More Praise for Green D

'An important book for everyo
fellow believers are doing to ᵤ﹍ ﹍
will gain a more complete and accurate picture of how Islam sees ᵤᵣₑ
world.'

—Imam Siraj Wahaj, Masjid Al-Taqwa, Brooklyn, New York

'Green Deen adds new thinking and allies to help solve the persistent social, energy, and infrastructure challenges that we all face as a planet, as nations, and in our own communities, every day.'

—Majora Carter, founder, The Majora Carter Group, cohost of Sundance Channel's *The Green*, and host of NPR's *The Promised Land*

'Green Deen connects faith to environment to social justice. It's a guide for all of us trying to save people and the planet.'

—Rami Nashashibi, Executive Director, Inner-City Muslim Action Network

'While there are many belief systems on this planet, few have been as deeply maligned as Islam in recent years. In that context, it is a beautiful and powerful call that Ibrahim Abdul-Matin puts out to his community and to the world, crying out that within Islam are the very tenets which are needed to save the world—for Muslims and non-Muslims. It is an act of faith to be sustainable...that is the essential truth which this book teaches us all.'

—Adrienne Maree Brown, Executive Director, The Ruckus Society

'Ibrahim Abdul-Matin is one of the premier scholars and practitioners joining the green economy to Islam. His work reminds environmentalism of the spirituality in deep ecology and provides a pathway for an economic system to work within a framework of reverence.'

—Nikki Henderson, Executive Director, People's Grocery

'Is this a Muslim book about the environment, an environmental book about Islam, or a poem and a prayer to the unity of all creation? It is all of these and more—*Green Deen* is a stunning hybrid creation from an extraordinary and wise new literary voice. Please welcome Ibrahim Abdul-Matin, black American and Muslim, to the pantheon of important environmental writers.'

—**William Upski Wimsatt, founder, League of Young Voters, and author of** *Please Don't Bomb the Suburbs*

'*Green Deen* shows how the authentic religious values and practices of Islam should lead to a wholesome, healthy, and compassionate lifestyle that benefi ts all living things. Abdul-Matin writes in accessible, intelligent, and motivating language, making this an excellent book for all readers.'

—**Ingrid Mattson, PhD, President, The Islamic Society of North America, and Director, The Duncan Black Macdonald Center for the Study of Islam and Christian-Muslim Relations at Hartford Seminary**

Green
Deen

Green Deen

What Islam Teaches About Protecting The Planet

IBRAHIM ABDUL-MATIN

KUBE
PUBLISHING

First published in England by Kube Publishing Ltd.

Kube Publishing Ltd.
Markfield Conference Centre
Ratby Lane, Markfield
Leicestershire LE67 9SY
Tel: +44 (0) 1530 249230. Fax: +44 (0) 1530 249656
Website: www.kubepublishing.com
Email: info@kubepublishing.com

Distributed in the UK, the Middle East and North Africa by Kube
Publishing Ltd.

First published in the United States by Berrett-Koehler Publishers in 2010.

ISBN: 978-1-84774-040-3 paperback

A CIP data record for this book is available from the British Library.

I dedicate this book to

My parents
Khadijah Matin, Ishmawil K. Abdul-Matin, and Auntie Amina

My siblings
Karim Jr., Jehan, Adilah, Tauhirah, and Ali

In loving memory of my grandparents
Samuel Graham Nixon Sr. and Lena Bailey Nixon
William Gaitha Pegg Sr. and Wilma Hayes Pegg

My wife
Fatima Ashraf

O You who have set out on the path of inner development, do not read my book only as a poetical work, or a book of magic, but read it with understanding; and for this a man must be hungry for something, dissatisfied with himself and this world.

—*Farid al-Din Attar*

Contents

x   Contents

KEITH ELLISON

U.S. Congressman,
Minnesota Fifth Congressional District

The seeds of this book were sown at a meeting of the 2008 Congressional Black Caucus in Washington, DC. Congressman André Carson and I had convened a session focusing on Muslim American communities and their development of a civic identity and expanding social activism. A young Green For All fellow, Ibrahim Abdul-Matin, was in the audience, and he convinced me to put on a green hard hat and have my picture taken with a poster saying "We're Ready for Green Jobs Now!" It was part of a national campaign with the goal of solving two of the greatest problems of this generation: joblessness and the assault on the environment. Ibrahim made an important connection that day—that the faith community needs to be involved in the green movement.

Solving problems is about making the right connections. I remember making the connection between the excessive number of asthma cases in my community and the coal-fired power plant a few blocks away. But it wasn't until I ran for the Minnesota state legislature for the first time that it really clicked for me.

I was standing outside a local elementary school in 2002, talking with a public health nurse who told me that we had a chance to convert that coal-fired power plant to natural gas. She hastened to add that the natural gas–fired plant would still involve the use of a fossil fuel, but that high-efficiency natural gas–fired power stations can produce up to 70 percent fewer greenhouse gas emissions than existing coal-fired generators.

On the spot, we agreed to pull together a community meeting in the basement of a local Urban League building. To my surprise, a lot of people really wanted to help. I thought that most neighbours, many of whom were low- to moderate-income folks, would be more focused on job creation and public safety. But these folks saw a clean environment as key to their health, well-being, and safety.

People wanted a cleaner environment, and they wanted jobs connected to the cleaner environment. We agreed that we needed a vehicle, an organisation to channel our efforts around the coal-to-gas conversion. We called ourselves the Environmental Justice Advocates of Minnesota (EJAM). We didn't have any experts, but we had a lot of folks with heart and passion.

EJAM invited the Public Utilities Commission, the agency charged with approving the coal-to-gas conversion, to hold a hearing in the same Urban League building where we'd held our first meeting. Two hundred and fifty people came. One older man walked up to the microphone, hoisted a string of fish into the air, and lamented the loss of edible fish because of the mercury contamination caused by the coal plant. The public health nurse who talked me into organising around the coal plant conversion brought in a banker's box full of asthma inhalers. She said they were from the kids at the elementary school. By time the hearing ended, folks had expressed their views about a cleaner environment. These people were not the usual suspects—the lawyers, the scientists, the industry types. They were 'We the People'—kids and pensioners, African Americans and whites, Hmong and Somali, Latino and more. They were Muslims, Christians and Jews, Hindus and others. All were joined together with the simple idea that all people should have the right to drink clean water, breathe clean air, and help make the rules that govern our environment.

The Public Utilities Commission (PUC) decided to move ahead and approve the coal-to-gas conversion, and PUC leaders pointed to our public hearing as one of the main turning points in that struggle. As a result, kids and adults today in Minneapolis can breathe easier, and grandfathers might one day be able to eat the fish they catch with their grandchildren.

EJAM helped make the connections between hardworking people and environmental justice. An EJAM organiser, Karen Monahan, made the connection between me and Ibrahim—a young Muslim politico who was writing about Islam and the environment. Soon I realised that Ibrahim was the guy I'd met at the 2008 caucus who'd taken the photo of me in the green hard hat. Like the work we have done through EJAM, *Green Deen* brings faith communities into the environmental movement by changing the conversation from the facts of global warming to the fact that we all live and work here together and have a collective responsibility to keep this place clean and safe for everyone.

Ibrahim is a man of faith, as many Americans are. In

Green Deen, he talks to the same people who started EJAM — Muslims, Christians, Jews, Hindus, Buddhists, environmentalists, and many others who all see the value in the simple ideas that drove us to create a coalition in my home state of Minnesota. We learned that environmental advocacy is not only the prerogative of the experts, politicians, and the industry executives. Ordinary citizens can impact environmental policy, and Ibrahim reminds people of faith that their impact is important and very much needed.

We the people can and must shape environmental policy. We can make the connections.

Bismillah ar-Rahman ar-Rahim—
In the Name of Allah, the Most Beneficent, Most Merciful

This Deen Called Islam

Most people are aware of a global religion called Islam. Islam is a *Deen*—Arabic for a religion, a path, a way of life. Islam means submission to the will of the One God, Allah. *Allah* is the Arabic word for God, just as the Spanish word for God is *Dios*. Allah is the God of Judaism, Christianity, and Islam. By focusing on One Creator, Islam allows humankind the opportunity to be one and to have a common purpose. Muslims believe that Islam is the final expression of the same message that came earlier to the Jews, the Christians, and other mono-theistic believers. For Muslims, the revelations prior to the Qur'an are essentially part of a larger canon of understanding. This is why, in Arabic, Christians and Jews are referred to as Ahl al-Kitab, 'people of the book'. Islam recognizes the existence and the legitimacy of other spiritual paths and teaches mutual understanding, respect, and focus on similarities as a means to bring people together, not push them apart.

The final revelation, the Qur'an, consists of directives, beliefs, manners, behaviours, and stories intended to guide humanity. Some are tied to certain incidents. Others are tied to human nature. Still others are about everyday life, including advice on eating healthily, preserving water, and conducting business. The Qur'an today is the same as it was fourteen hundred years ago, when Muslims believe it was revealed by God to the Prophet Muhammad (peace be upon him).

The Prophet Muhammad (peace be upon him) was a messenger of God. Muslims believe that he was the last messenger in the line of messengers from Adam to Jesus. He was a human being, flesh and blood, just like the rest of us. He was born in the city of Mecca in Saudi Arabia in 570 CE. He worked as a merchant. He married and had children. For his entire life, he was known as 'al-Amin', 'The Trustworthy'. At the age of forty, he began to contemplate the meaning of life. He retreated into a cave on the side of a mountain, where he began to receive revelation from God. He was commanded by Allah to share this message with the people of Arabia— exactly as it was revealed and also through acting according to its teachings. The teachings—the actions and the sayings— of the Prophet Muhammad (peace be upon him) are known as the sunnah; collectively they are known as the hadith. Muslims follow the Qur'an and the hadith in their practice of Islam.

Muslims also follow the Five Pillars of Islam: faith in One God, five daily prayers, giving charity, fasting during the holy month of Ramadan, and making the pilgrimage, or Hajj, to Mecca. The Oneness of God affirms that everything is connected to God—that we and everything on Earth are all part of the same fabric of creation. The five daily prayers take place at set times: sunrise, midday, late afternoon, sunset, and nighttime. Giving charity means donating a portion of your saved earnings to feeding or supporting those less fortunate. Fasting during the thirty days of the month of Ramadan means abstaining from food, drink, and sexual intimacy from sunrise to sunset each day. The Hajj is a journey in which Muslims from all over the world stand side by side at Mecca to affirm their belief in One God. The Hajj takes place annually, and for Muslims it is a religious duty to make the journey at least once in a lifetime if they are able to do so.

Muslims also live by ethical principles that guide how they interact with the world. In this book I look at six of these principles as they apply to our relationship to the environment: understanding the Oneness of God and His creation (*tawhid*), seeing signs of God (*ayat*) everywhere, being a steward (*khalifah*) of the Earth, honouring the trust we have with God (*amanah*) to be protectors of the planet, moving toward justice (*adl*), and living in balance with nature (*mizan*). These principles are the rubric upon which I am determining what constitutes a Green Deen—that is, living and practising Islam while also honouring the environmental ethos of Islam.

Why I Am Writing This Book

Let me be honest—dozens of people are likely more qualified than I to write on this intersection of environmentalism and Islam. In fact, in writing this book, I met many of them. You might be one of those scholars or Muslim environmentalists yourself. The reason I decided to write *Green Deen* is because I come with a set of experiences that uniquely situate me to see how being an environmentalist and protecting the planet are deeply imbedded in the Muslim tradition from a variety of perspectives.

At the core, I am a networker and organiser. From the beginning, I have seen this book as a conversation starter among people of faith, environmentalists, organisers, youth, elders, religious scholars, and everyone in between about the role faith can play in the larger environmental movement. Because of my diverse work experiences, because I've lived in several cities around the United States, and because my activism has taken me outside the United States as well, I have built a network that includes a broad spectrum of people.

I am the Muslim child of community activist converts to Islam. I am a seeker, and for the past ten years, I have sought a deeper understanding of my religion, my Deen, and have grown in my practise. A native New Yorker, I moved to California to absorb wisdom from Zaytuna College and to develop my relationship with Allah. I am also a lover of the environment, and my career has reflected this. I started off as director of youth programmes at Prospect Park in Brooklyn. I helped create the Brooklyn Academy of Science and the Environment, a new public high school that's seen much success. I served as an Outward Bound instructor on Thompson Island in Boston Harbor, helping young people develop an appreciation of themselves and the planet. Additionally, my work in the social justice community has taken me all over the United States as I worked alongside youth organisers and activists seeking to transform their local and regional communities.

Returning to New York, I acquired a master's degree in public administration, with a focus on environmental policy, and consulted for several green jobs programmes, including Green For All in Oakland, California, and Green City Force in my hometown of Brooklyn, New York. Today, I proudly work in the New York City Mayor's Office as a policy adviser on issues of long-term planning and sustainability. I am always developing and perfecting my Green Deen, and this book represents the people, places, and events that have shaped my understanding of Islam and my role as a steward of the Earth.

What This Book Is Not

This book is not an analysis of all of the verses in the Qur'an and all of the hadith of the Prophet Muhammad (peace be upon him) related to the environment. I will not engage in interpretation (*tafsir*) of the Holy Book—I am not qualified in this regard. So, no, I am not a foremost scholar who will offer you a stellar critique of environmental policy and its implications for the followers of Islam. This book is also not an exhaustive review of the environmental policies in Muslim countries around the globe. Although I touch on international examples, the focus is on the United States. I am, after all, a Muslim American.

What This Book Is

This book is a collection of thoughts, stories, analyses, and practical pieces of advice to help anyone looking to further their Green Deen—living and practising Islam while honouring the principles that connect humans to protecting the planet. I am a Muslim with a deeply personal relationship to the Qur'an and the hadith. Like most people of faith, I have spent much time reflecting on scripture, reciting its words,

seeking to understand its spirit and to live out its commandments in a way that makes sense for my life. For example, a
well-known hadith relates that the Prophet Muhammad
(peace be upon him), when eating, ate from the dish closest
to him. I have heard this hadith many times in my life, but
as I delved deeper into developing my own Green Deen, it
occurred to me that the spirit of this hadith could also be used
to encourage people to buy food from local sources. I have
interpreted the spirit of other hadith similarly, as you will see
reflected in this book.

I am an American whose roots go back to the Revolutionary
War, and this book is therefore inevitably centred on people
and places in North America. I do not mean to suggest that
only Muslim Americans can have a Green Deen—anyone can
have a Green Deen. I am simply presenting the perspective I
know from being born and raised in the United States, and I
hope these domestic examples will resonate with people living
in other countries as well.

Muslim Americans come from all over the world. They
are a diverse community, hailing from Afghanistan, Albania,
Algeria, Bangladesh, Egypt, Ghana, Guinea, Guyana, India,
Indonesia, Iran, Iraq, Ivory Coast, Jordan, Malaysia, Morocco,
Pakistan, Palestine, Saudi Arabia, Senegal, Sierra Leone,
Somalia, Sudan, Syria, Turkey, the United Arab Emirates, and
Yemen—and this is by no means an exhaustive list. Islam in
America exemplifies 'staying local, going global'.

Though Muslims come from all parts of the world, our
common mode of communication is Arabic, the language of
the Qur'an. In some parts of this book I will transliterate.
This is my humble attempt to connect with non-Muslims, as

well as Muslims who may not be fluent in Arabic or familiar with some of the terms I use. I have also provided a glossary of Islamic terms at the end of the book.

How This Book Is Organised

This book is organised into four parts, each dealing with one of today's major environmental problems: waste, watts (energy), water, and food. Each section presents the problem, offers solutions in the form of individual stories of Muslims who are living a Green Deen, and includes specific *ayah*s (verses) from the Qur'an and specific hadith that support a Green Deen.[1] I also tell stories from my own life and include my personal feelings about particular *ayah*s and hadith to clarify a problem or to support a particular solution.

The core purpose and heart of this book is to build a movement that brings together spiritual practice with protection of the environment.

In part I, 'Waste', I examine the politics of overconsumption. Chapter 1, 'The Problem of Overconsumption', focuses on our fixation with 'things' and with buying more and more of them, the negative effects of this overconsumption on people's psyches, and how it generates a system of waste and toxicity that is polluting the planet.

In chapter 2, 'The Environmental Movement as a Response to Overconsumption', I examine the history of the environmental movement and its present-day response to overconsumption and discuss how the principles of Islam are deeply woven into what many see as a secular movement.

Chapter 3, 'Green Muslims', highlights Muslim Americans

who are living a Green Deen. Some are pioneers and inno-
vators, some are organisers, and others are families just trying to survive and live a faith-based life in harmony with the
environment. This chapter is designed to inspire you and get
you thinking about what you can do to move toward living a
Green Deen.

In chapter 4, 'Green Mosques', I look at what makes a
Green Mosque, from the carbon footprint of the building
itself to the everyday practises of the people who use it—and
the effect of each on the planet. Included are examples of
Green Mosques in Abu Dhabi, Singapore, and England.

Part II, 'Watts', deals with energy. In chapter 5, 'Energy
from Hell', I review energy sources that cause our carbon
footprint to grow. All these energy sources—coal, gas, and
oil—come from the ground, so I call them 'Energy from Hell'.
In contrast, chapter 6, 'Energy from Heaven', examines two
renewable energy sources—the sun and the wind—that come
from the sky.

Chapter 7, 'Efficiency and Green Jobs', discusses how green
jobs and a green economy have the potential to transition our
society from an economic system that is reliant on pollution
to one that is cleaner and greener and that fulfills our responsibility as stewards of the Earth.

In chapter 8, 'Living Off the Grid', through the story of a
community of Muslims in Chiapas, Mexico, I remind us that
there is another alternative to energy efficiency: living off the
main electrical grid and not relying on centralised power.

Part III, 'Water', takes a look at how essential water is to
life, yet how scarce clean, fresh water has become in today's
world. Chapter 9, 'Water—Essential for Survival', is my water

manifesto. It sets the stage for the discussion and the activism that need to take place around water.

Chapter 10, 'Toxic Waste in Our Water', discusses how water sources have been polluted and, in some cases, destroyed by industrial and corporate practises. Here I tell the story of my own sister, Tauhirah Abdul-Matin, who has dedicated her life and career to testing water for toxicity.

Chapter 11, 'The Wonderful World of Wudu', looks at how water can be conserved in the performance of wudu—the ablutions Muslims make in preparation for each of the five daily prayers.

Part IV, 'Food', is all about food. It is often said, 'You are what you eat', which implies that the cleaner, healthier, and more natural your food, the cleaner, healthier, and more natural you are. Food is so important that I present it with the utmost care and lots of stories.

In chapter 12, 'Feeding Your Family', I look at the Islamic standard of *halal* (permissible) food and at families who have made ethical choices in feeding their families. Chapter 13, 'Urban and Suburban Food Gardens', offers detailed examples of productive gardens in each setting.

In chapter 14, 'The Farmers' Market', I focus on Qaid Hassan, a young entrepreneur who brings produce to low-income communities in Chicago's inner city. Chapter 15, 'Green Dhabihah', presents a case for green dhabihah—meat prepared in an Islamically lawful way.

Finally, in chapter 16, 'American Halal—Setting the Stage for the Future', I look at the contributions of an organic and halal pioneer Adnan Durrani.

At the end of the book you will also find a glossary of the

Islamic terms used throughout, as well as a list of resources to help you further your education and involvement in the Green Deen movement if you desire.

In these times, Islam is a fixture in the media for many reasons—but what do most people really know about the religion of 1.4 billion people on the planet? Even Muslims need a refresher sometimes to understand the simplicity of their faith—of any faith for that matter. We are all here to take care of the planet and of one another. Islam has a plan for that. Our Deen is a living, vibrant tradition with roots in stewardship.

As I have mentioned, I am not a scholar of Qur'an and hadith. I am not a theologian. My upbringing was rooted in appreciation for the environment, in eating clean and pure foods, and in being a responsible person who takes care of self, others, and the planet. I was raised to think that leaving the Earth a better place than we found it is a mandate from God. My personal relationship with Allah has developed into one in which I take responsibility for everything the Earth gives me and for what I give back to the Earth. I believe that Muslims can strengthen their spirituality, become more active in their communities, and live better lives by living a Green Deen.

How green is your Deen?

The Earth Is a Mosque

The Earth is a mosque, and everything in it is sacred. I learned this basic tenet of Islam from my father. He was raised in New York City in the borough of Queens, spent summers in Virginia, and always loved and respected the natural world. He took it upon himself to share this appreciation with his children. I spent my early childhood in the New York boroughs of Queens and Brooklyn. My brother and I used to think the entire world was a sea of concrete buildings. My father upended that reality the day he took us to Bear Mountain. Just north of New York City, Bear Mountain is known as a hiker's paradise. On that trip, we were black Muslim city kids hiking in "the country" for the first time. What I recall from that day was moss growing on rocks, mushrooms on rotting wood, and drinking from my first carton of juice — the kind you poke a straw into.

When it was time for the afternoon prayer, my father stopped to pray. My brother and I asked him where he was going to pray. He pointed to the ground, to a small area he had brushed free of twigs and leaves. Until that day, prayer for us had always been something done at home or in the mosque.

Our mosque, Masjid At-Taqwa, was an oasis of Islam in the heart of the struggling Bedford-Stuyvesant neighbourhood (better known as Bed-Stuy) of Brooklyn. The imam of Masjid At-Taqwa, the respected Siraj Wahaj, later became the first Muslim to give the opening prayer in a session of Congress.[1] My father was one of the first twenty-five brothers involved in building Masjid At-Taqwa. To us, the mosque meant proud black families creating community and praying together.

On Bear Mountain, as we prepared to kneel down in prayer, my father related a hadith, a saying of the Prophet Muhammad (peace be upon him): 'Wherever you may be at the time of prayer, you may pray, for it (the Earth) is all a mosque.'[2] At that instant, and I could not have been more than five or six years old, I understood for the first time: the Earth is a mosque; a mosque is sacred; therefore, the Earth is sacred. That moment of prayer on the mountain, thanks to the hadith my father relayed, transformed the way that I would see the world forever.

As an adult, my contemplation of the notion that the Earth is a mosque led to my discovery of the core message of this book—that Islam, the world's second-largest religion, provides a helpful lens to prompt action among Muslims and anyone else concerned about saving the Earth. This lens encompasses a variety of principles—understanding the Oneness of God and His creation (*tawhid*); seeing signs of God everywhere (*ayat*); being a steward of the Earth (*khalifah*); honouring the covenant, or trust, we have with God (*amanah*) to be protectors of the planet; moving toward justice (*adl*); and living in balance with nature (*mizan*). Each of these principles points to the same well-kept secret: that Islam teaches a deep love of the planet, because loving the planet means loving ourselves and loving our Creator. That is to say, Islam teaches that we are all One. 'The Earth is a mosque' is another way of saying that we are all part of the same, wonderful fabric of creation.

What Is a 'Green Deen'?

In Arabic, 'Deen' is defined as a religion or creed, a faith or belief, a path or a way.[3] Christianity is a Deen. Judaism is a Deen. Buddhism is a Deen. Islam is a Deen. The Holy Book of Islam is the Qur'an. In the Qur'an there is a surah, or chapter, that directly speaks to 'those who reject faith.' This surah, known as the 'Al-Kafirun', or 'The Rejecters of Faith', has an *ayah,* or verse, that says:

> To you then be your way and to me mine. (Qur'an 109:6)

In Arabic, this *ayah* is read as 'lakum deenukum wa li al-deen.' It is often cited to illustrate that Islam, the religion of 1.4 billion human beings,[4] is, like all things, a choice.

A Green Deen is the choice to practise the religion of Islam while affirming the integral relationship between faith and the environment, or, better said, the natural world, the universe, and all that is in it. I recently listened to Yasir Syeed—whom I will talk about in greater detail in chapter 15, 'Green Dhabihah'—who said, 'What we have as Muslims is comprehensive. It is a living tradition that is spiritually nourishing and intellectually coherent.'[5]

Islam is what motivates me to be a steward of the Earth. But this role is not limited to me. In Islam, all humans are considered stewards of the Earth, and in the Qur'an, God sets forward clear principles about this stewardship that include taking care of oneself, of others, and of the planet.[6]

These Islamic teachings can be useful to all people who are concerned about protecting the planet. It makes plain sense for advocates of the Earth to know what Islam says and what Muslims are doing and can do to be part of the larger environmental movement. As I discovered in the writing of this book, there are many people of all faiths actively involved in the protection of the planet, using their faith as their organising principle. Harnessing this passion with the passion of those who are drawn to the environmental movement for other reasons makes the overall movement to protect the planet, animals, people, and plants a stronger movement that represents the diversity of the planet.

Islam and the Environment

A Green Deen is both a spiritual and a scientific path. One of the least understood facts about Islam is that it is quite compatible with science. There is no competition between religion and science. God, through messengers and scripture, has given humans a clear directive to take care of the Earth. This directive is both spiritual and scientific. Through science, we come to know more about creation and how to best take care of it.

Science appears in the *ayah*s (verses) of the Qur'an, such as those describing the oceans meeting and not mixing,[7] or the development of a foetus.[8] The compatibility of Islam and science is important because much evidence showing that we have been polluting and negatively affecting the planet comes from scientific enquiry. For years, scientific evidence has been telling us that our choices have led to rampant pollution and climate change. Too much carbon in the atmosphere has led to a steady rise in global temperatures.[9] Those who deny climate change have asserted that it is hubris for humans to think they can change what God has already created. In Islam, however, God clearly tells humans that they can have an impact on what He has created—and He provides guidance on how to make this impact a positive one.

The Six Principles of a Green Deen

The conviction that the Earth is a mosque is rooted in some core ethical Islamic principles that we should comprehend when attempting to live a Green Deen. In order to grasp Islam's commitment to the Oneness of all things (and how this commitment can be used to advocate for the environment), it's helpful to understand some of the core spiritual principles and practices that align Islam and the environment so closely. These ethical principles, which many scholars of Islam have studied and discussed, were recently codified and presented to me by Faraz Khan, a brilliant young scholar of Islam and the environment.[10] They are:

1. Understanding the Oneness of God and His creation (*tawhid*)
2. Seeing signs of God (*ayat*) everywhere
3. Being a steward (*khalifah*) of the Earth
4. Honouring the covenant, or trust, we have with God (*amanah*) to be protectors of the planet
5. Moving toward justice (*adl*)
6. Living in balance with nature (*mizan*)

Understanding the Oneness of God and His Creation (*Tawhid*)

Living a Green Deen means understanding that everything comes from Allah. We recognise that Allah is the Creator and sustainer of everything. Allah says in the Qur'an:

> He is the First and the Last, the Evident and the Hidden: and He has full knowledge of all things. (Qur'an 57:3).

We come from Allah, and so does the universe and everything in it. Everything emanates from the same source. If you look at the smallest particle that human beings can see using the most powerful magnification, you see the building blocks of atoms: protons, neutrons, and electrons. They look like small flashes of light. Now, if you turn your gaze into the farthest reaches of the universe, you see what looks eerily similar—quasars. They are the most distant objects we can see, and they, too, look like small flashes of light. That light is an expression of the Oneness of Allah and His creation (*tawhid*). For at the elemental, spiritual, and scientific levels, everything is comprised of the same basic elements—little flashes of light. The universe is aglow with continuity. A Green Deen understands and looks to follow the signs that speak to this connectivity.

Seeing Signs of God (*Ayat*) Everywhere

Living a Green Deen means seeing everything in the natural world as a sign (*ayah*) of our Creator. 'Signs for those who reflect' is a constant refrain in the Qur'an. Signs from the Creator are all around us. To treat the natural world poorly means to deny the signs of our Creator. In Arabic, the word *ayah* can refer to one of the 6,236 verses of the Qur'an, or the same word can mean the signs around us—the mountains, the trees, the seas.

These signs are evidence of God. We only need to expand our vision to see everything through this lens. When we are walking in nature, we can see these signs as the trees, the wind, the birds, and the waves in a body of water. Reflecting on these signs, we can learn about ourselves and about the reality of the connectivity that is at the core of Islam. When we are reading the Qur'an, we can think of ourselves as taking an existential walk through nature—we can fine-tune our attention to see every aspect of creation as being a divine message.

What we see in Allah's signs is also a reflection of what we are intrinsically. When we stand on a mountaintop or at the edge of a great sea or watch a glorious sunrise, we are immersed in the amazement of the signs Allah has spread out before us. These experiences can lead us into a state of awe. Our awe is our sense that we are part of the amazing beauty of those signs.

Being a Steward (*Khalifah*) of the Earth

Living a Green Deen means understanding that God created us directly from the Earth and that we must do all that we can to take care of it, protect it, and manage all of its bounty in a sustainable way. We all have a blessed beginning, and we will all come back to Allah at the end of our time here on Earth. Will we leave the planet better than we found it? Those who do so are stewards (*khalifah*) of the Earth.

Human beings are made from the Earth and are the representatives of God on Earth. Humans, according to Islam, are considered the best of God's creation. We have been blessed with intellect and reason. In Islam, there are different forms of creation. Humans are one. Angels are another. Humans were made from clay collected from throughout Earth. This clay was then infused with the *fitrah,* 'the essence of Allah'. From these raw materials, Earth, water, and a divine spirit, Allah formed humans.[11]

Because the Earth is the essence of our being, it is our responsibility to protect it. When we die, we will be resurrected in both body and spirit and will be held to account for all that we've done for ourselves, others, and the planet. This is the essence of the *khalifah,* Arabic for 'steward'. We are all stewards of the Earth. We are perfectly created to be able to live and thrive here. The Prophet Muhammad (peace be upon him) declared: 'The world is beautiful and verdant, and verily Allah, be He exalted, has made you His stewards in it, as He sees how you acquit yourselves.'[12] Although I am no scholar, I have a personal relationship to the sacred texts, and I understand this saying to be a reminder of two truths: that we have bounty all around us and that we have a deep relationship with our Creator. The question is: What will we do with it? Will we respectfully manage this bounty by honouring the covenant we have with God to be his stewards?

Honouring the Trust We Have with God (*Amanah*)

We have a 'trust' (*amanah*) on this Earth, a sacred covenant with our Creator. Following a Green Deen means knowing that we are entrusted by God to act as stewards of the Earth. This trust is a promise to protect the planet, and it comes with the gifts of speech, knowledge, and the freedom to make decisions. God has given us the ability to make decisions over the land and the animals, and He trusts us to be responsible with this gift. We can choose to cooperate with nature—or not. We can choose to be inspired or burdened by this trust with Allah. Either way, we will be held accountable for our actions.

Some have taken the solemn trust with God and our role as stewards of the Earth to mean that we can do whatever we want without consequence. They push limits until their actions harm the natural world, all in pursuit of material gain. Islam teaches otherwise—it teaches that the Earth is a sacred place. When we impose our will on the Earth, we risk polluting it. Our trust from God is not a licence to pillage and destroy or to take from others—be they animals, plants, the ground, or the sky—without a just return. Our mandate from God dictates that we must praise the Creator, take care of the planet, and take care of one another.

Moving Toward Justice (*Adl*)

Treating the Earth like a mosque means treating the natural world in a just and fair manner (*adl*). We must accept our role as the protectors of the planet, a planet that has come under assault from the actions of humankind in pursuit of economic gain. The environmental justice and climate justice movements have come as a response to protect the planet and to protect the people who bear the brunt of pollution and climate change.

Those seeking to live a Green Deen should understand that communities without control of political and economic power often suffer disproportionately the negative effects of environmental pollution and environmental degradation. These communities are also less able to make a living wage from the resources available in their locale.[13]

Our economic system is partly to blame for this injustice. For far too long it has been based on a model of economic growth by any means necessary. In this system, the Earth is not seen as a mosque; it is not considered sacred. Instead, the natural world is viewed as an opportunity for resource extraction. We assault our planet and view people as an afterthought in our collective pursuit of expansive markets and the search for natural resources to create more goods.

A Green Deen that is just recognises that people can have a negative impact on the planet. This conviction is clearly stated in the Qur'an:

> Corruption has appeared on the land and in the sea because of what the hands of humans have wrought. This is in order that we give them a taste of the consequences of their misdeeds that perhaps they will turn to the path of right guidance. (Qur'an 30:41)

The American-born Islamic scholar Imam Zaid Shakir observes of this verse: 'The earliest commentators on the Qur'an have described this corruption as the drying up of the rains, the disappearance of the harvest of the sea, and other ecologically relevant meanings.'[14] This quote shows that there is evidence in the Qur'an of humans impacting negatively the planet.

To really live as though everything is connected, we need to examine how our actions are affecting the land, the sea, and the people and animals who live on the Earth. Is our approach in concordance with this Oneness? By moving toward a just economy and a just way of life, we move away from the wanton exploitation of land and sea, as well as of people and animals, and turn instead toward a way of life that affirms the abundance in creation. Our actions are not focussed on fighting for limited resources, but rather on ensuring that everyone has equal access to these resources. While pursuing a Green Deen does not ensure equality of outcomes, it can advance a framework that ensures that people, animals, plants, and all of God's creation are seen as irrevocably connected. By recognising this connection, harming people and animals, and the air, land, and sea in the process of creating and sustaining wealth will be reduced, if not eliminated.

Living in Balance with Nature (*Mizan*)

Everything in creation is made to exist in a perfect balance (*mizan*). Seeing the Earth as a mosque means respecting this balance. Think of the sun and the moon, which give us night and day. For thousands of years we have been able to use this balanced system to raise our crops and to know when to sleep, work, and pray. Islam provides evidence of an omnipotent God who has properly made humans for the environment. He has ordered the stars and planets into fixed orbits. He has made an invisible energy field—gravity—to keep everything in its place on Earth. He has made plants and animals our friends, protectors, and sustenance. God asserts His balance in the Qur'an:

> He has created man: He has taught him speech and Intelligence. The sun and the moon follow courses (exactly) computed. And the herbs and the trees—both (alike) bow in adoration. And the Firmament has He raised high, and He has set up the Balance of (Justice). In order that you may not transgress (due) balance. So establish weight with justice and fall not short in the balance. It is He who has spread out the earth for (His) creatures. (Qur'an 55:3–10).

Everything has been ordered into this delicate balance that God speaks of in the Qur'an. Justice in Islam is in maintaining this balance.

As mentioned previously, reflecting on this balance is a form of worship. 'Signs for those who reflect' is a constant refrain in the Qur'an. So we reflect on what we see in the world around us. Today it is clear that human beings have affected the balance of the natural world. The Qur'an says:

> So set your face steadily and truly to the Faith: (establish) Allah's handiwork according to the pattern on which he has made mankind: No change (let there be) in the work (wrought) by Allah: that is the true Religion: But most among mankind understand not. (Qur'an 30:30)

Islam teaches humanity not to disturb the balance.

Greening Your Deen Through Prayer

You must pray! Living a Green Deen means opening your heart to the possibility of understanding the Oneness of God and His creation (*tawhid*); seeing the signs of God everywhere (*ayat*); being a steward of the Earth (*khalifah*); honouring the trust we have from God to be protectors of the planet (*amanah*); moving toward justice (*adl*); and living in balance with nature (*mizan*). We open our hearts first and foremost through prayer. Prayer is the key means by which we pursue our Deen on a daily basis. The creations on Earth pray all the time. Animals and plants exist in a state of remembrance of the All-Mighty as the Holy Book notes:

> And the herbs and trees—both (alike) bow in adoration. (Qur'an 55:6)

A Green Deen starts with self-reflection. We need to 'get right' within ourselves in order to treat the Earth as the sacred place that it is. For me, for Muslims, prayer is key, as it allows us to organise our day around the remembrance of Allah and at the same time be in the same rhythm as the planet Earth. Others might achieve this rhythm through meditation, contemplation, or love, or perhaps your prayer encompasses all of these.

If everything in nature is in a constant state of prayer, then prayer for a human being is the start of physical and spiritual expression of this Oneness. As an adult, I have had the fortune of travelling across the United States, and I am always connecting with open spaces in the natural world. Prayer has been the link across all these spaces. I pray everywhere, from alongside Highway 50 in Nevada to the edge of the Pacific Ocean in Marin County. In Hawaii, with my feet deep in black sand, I have prayed listening to the constant sound of the crashing waves, I have prayed after swimming with sea turtles, and I have cleansed myself before prayer with lush rainwater runoff. I have braved blizzards in Chicago, hiked mountains in Vermont, and climbed quartz monzonite rock formations in California's Joshua Tree National Park—all the while finding time and place to pray. My experiences have shown me that the Earth truly is a mosque.

To manifest a Green Deen, we need to begin as our Prophet Muhammad (peace be upon him) instructed us: by healing our hearts. In a recent lecture the noted scholar Tariq Ramadan said, 'It is not because you are poor that you are good. It is not because you are rich that you are bad. It is what is in your heart.'[15] The Holy Prophet (peace be upon him) said: 'Verily, there is in the body a piece of flesh, that if it is correct, the rest of the body will be correct due to it, and if it is corrupt, then the rest of the body will be corrupt due to it. Verily, it is the heart.'[16] Our hearts need healing just as our planet needs healing. We can heal through prayer, and we can heal the planet through prayer—not just in the spiritual sense, but also by becoming more open to living a life in concert with all of creation. The way we treat the planet is a reflection of how we treat ourselves, and the way we treat ourselves is a reflection of how we treat our planet.

Building the Green Deen Movement

Once we have begun walking a Green Deen and healing our hearts through prayer, the next step is building a movement—you can call it a Green Deen movement—and connect that to the green interfaith movement, and connect that to the environmental justice and traditional environmental movements, and connect that to the human rights movement, and connect that to the human movement. We all need to reflect. As Winona LaDuke, former Green Party vice-presidential candidate, put it at a Boston rally I attended in early 2000, collective action is required to 'renegotiate our relationship with the Earth'. Building a movement is part of living a Green Deen.

Islam is an active religion concerned with action on core ethical principles that are deeply congruent with a love of the planet. Following a Green Deen means following these principles, not only in our own personal lives, but also within our wider communities, and prompting these communities into action. We have a responsibility to join with others— to become one—as a community that lives a Green Deen, treating the Earth as a mosque. Encouragingly, Muslims and their environmental allies are already doing this all over the world. Indeed, all across the planet, Muslims are drawing on core Islamic principles to build a burgeoning Green Deen movement. I envision four actions to continue building this movement.

1. *We need to tell our stories.* This book presents stories of Muslims and other people of faith who have demonstrated by their actions that they are willing to be actively engaged in protecting the planet Earth. Their inspiring stories serve as a guide to living a Green Deen and show us how harmony can be built amongst all of creation. My hope is that, through these stories, you the reader will understand that we are, in fact, here with a purpose. I want you to be inspired by that purpose and the role that you can play.

2. *We need to get educated*—and to educate others—on the environmental issues and solutions. The way that people have managed the major systems of water, waste, energy, and food have defined civilisations throughout history. Let's look at some of the ways that water, waste, energy, and food have been emblematic of their times: The Romans built a famous aqueduct to bring water to cities. The spread of the bubonic plague was due, in large part, to the mismanagement of trash. The decision to use nuclear power for electricity defined the middle of the last century—for better and for worse. The management of food, for most of known history, has been done on a local scale—village to village, involving families and small local systems.

For better and for worse, we humans have tried our best to manage the resources we have, but we can and must do better. At no time in the history of the world have human beings been in more constant contact than we are now. This connectivity is a challenge and also a blessing. We can harness this people power to hold our institutions accountable and to find better ways to deliver water to the thirsty, food to the hungry, and power to the industrious—those with ambition, creativity, and ideas. We have to be the best stewards we can be, and we must find better ways to reduce the impact that our actions have on the planet.

3. *We need to connect with people of other faiths.* The beauty of living a Green Deen is that doing so enables us to know more about the world we live in and to connect with people of other faiths on a common platform. We are more powerful and more compassionate toward others when we realise that the Oneness and connectivity of life is the key to living a sustainable life. We know that the way we have been living is simply unsustainable.

The interfaith movement has generally been focussed on top-down interaction; however, the core commonality we all have is not in our understanding of what God is or is not, but in the fact that we all live together on Earth. Lay congregations can come together and do work. This work will consist of radically altering our way of thinking about development, profit, gain, and loss. Soon we will need to connect with those of other faiths to raise our children as part of a larger community of 'people of faith'. We make these connections for the sake of our children, because they learn from what they see more than from what we tell them.

One way to make such interfaith connections is through work—in community gardens, in Gulf cleanup efforts, in deconstructing old buildings and salvaging useful materials. Through work we form operational and emotional bonds that build community around our shared love of God and the planet. Service is the bond that connects people of all faiths. In the environmental movement, it will be incumbent upon Muslim, Christian, Jewish, and other faith congregants to connect in a spirit of service to our shared Earth.

4. *We need to be smart* — to try new ideas, and to be unafraid to fail. Advancing our collective Green Deen should not depend on the loudmouthing of any one priest or imam. Nor should it be the rabble-rousing of any one activist group or individual in a protest. Instead, this is a movement of ideas and creativity, a movement in which all participants can find ways in their home, mosque, and workplace to be more efficient in operating with less waste. Often what holds our communities back is a fear of failure. We should instead focus on the ultimate goals and the vision that has brought us to a realisation that we can be better representatives of God on the planet. Let us constantly remind ourselves that no human should go hungry or thirsty. All humans should be able to reasonate within the Oneness of creation and be the best they can be. The universe is aglow with continuity—we take this truth to be self-evident—we are all responsible for protecting the planet!

Part I Waste

Corruption has appeared on the land and in the sea because of what the hands of humans have wrought.
(Qur'an 30:41)

How do you relate to trash, to waste, to consumption? How do you understand the systems of production and consumption? Why do you consume? What do you consume? We live in a global world in which the tools and processes to sustain ourselves are all deeply connected.

A Green Deen is the choice to practise the religion of Islam while affirming the relationship between faith and the environment. As part of your personal Green Deen, for some period in your life, why not try doing without 'stuff'? No more cell phones and computers, no more packaged foods, nothing bought or sold at a chain store, nothing that has an on or off switch. No more paper or pens, no more cars and exhaust, just you. Just letting go and disconnecting from 'things'.

What kind of life would you have? It's okay to shrug your shoulders. A deeper question might be: What do you get out of all these things? Before we move forward, these are some critical questions to ask yourself—and it is okay if you do not have the answers. Imagine the time of the Prophet Muhammad (peace be upon him) and the simplicity in which he lived. Technologically, we've come a long way from the simple lives people lived fifteen hundred years ago, but that doesn't mean that the basic principles don't still ring true. The Prophet (peace be upon him) was a true steward of the planet (*khalifah*), and as the Messenger of Allah, he was the best example we have of being the *khalifah*, or the representative of Allah on Earth. He cared for plants and animals. He was a champion for and moved people toward justice (*adl*), and he advocated fairness in the marketplace. He embodied the verses (*ayat*) of the Qur'an in his speech, his manners, and his actions. When you think about your relationship to things, the material world, possessions, think of the greatest people—the ones we admire and honour. Did their achievements come about because of a focus on the material world or because of a focus on serving the world?

Sometimes I think we take a lot for granted. We also take the lessons of our Deen and how this tradition of ours can respond to the challenges we all face for granted. If one of the great lies of our age is that 'things' give us value, then the spiritual antidote is in developing your connection to God. One of the manifestations of this great lie that 'things' give us value is that we immerse ourselves in buying and consuming, no matter what the cost. What I describe as letting go of 'stuff' could be considered a retreat from the world but could also been seen as a direct action to counter that great lie. Things do not define us.

Retreating from the world is something Muslims just do not do. In our Deen, our religious path, we have been taught to be present in the world, to plan for this life and for the next. But to be in this world means to understand it, to be diligent, and to be informed. When dealing with waste, the essential question is not: What is waste? The essential question is: Where does it come from?

In this section on waste, I want you to think about your relationship to 'stuff' and 'things'. Of course, in doing so, you have to reflect on the Oneness of God and His creation (*tawhid*) and how all your actions affect everything around you. How did this 'stuff' and these 'things' transform from natural resources into what you now own? How did this 'thing' get from the manufacturer to you to the waste heaps that fill the forgotten corners of our globe? Could there be toxic waste seeping into the ground or into the air as a result of this 'stuff'? Allah entrusted the Earth to us, and this trust (*amanah*) is a sacred bond. Does our management of trash and waste represent honouring of this trust? If God ordered everything in perfect balance (*mizan*), does our management of waste, trash, and toxicity create imbalances?

We are all a part of this process, so it makes sense for us to educate ourselves on consumption, overconsumption, and the responses to each. I hope this section will assist you in rethinking what role you play in the trash and waste system.

Ask yourself: Where does your trash come from? Where does it go? How can you be actively involved in making the world a cleaner, less toxic place?

Chapter 1

The Problem of Overconsumption

Following a Green Deen and choosing to practise the religion of Islam while affirming the connection between faith and the environment begins, of course, through prayer. From there you can reflect on your relationship with God and with the planet and how you live in it.

I know it sounds funny, but let's begin with thinking about trash, what creates it, and the processes of consumption and overconsumption. Think of your first recollection of waste. When was the first time you became aware of trash? Each time I pose this question to an audience, the responses usually start out slow as people begin to work the idea over in their heads. I once put this question to a group of young Muslims in New York City—see which of their responses reasonates for you.

For Chris, it was when he was a child. Chris and his friends would collect aluminium cans and newspapers for money. They got $3 a pound for cans and $1 a pound for newspapers. He remembers learning for the first time that trash had value. Every day people work to move our trash, and governments pay to dump trash.

For Rami, it was as he was walking to the subway in Queens on his way to work one Monday morning. It was garbage pickup day, and there were stacks and stacks of garbage in front of every building. In the heat and humidity, the smell was unbearable. Rami threw up on his clothes and had to return home to change. He remembers thinking, 'I'm sure we can do better than this.' Of course we can, but we first have to know how things have been done in the past.

For Sadaf, it was seeing garbage bins on the Brooklyn Bridge overflowing with plastic bottles. It was a warm day, and a few metres away a man was selling bottled water. The vendor's customers were so thirsty, he couldn't keep up with their consumption, and all the empty bottles went into the trash.

For Jameela, it was when she was a child visiting Throggs Neck in the Bronx. She remembers seeing dead horseshoe crabs in the garbage can and saying to her dad, 'This isn't garbage.'

For Taha, it was seeing families picking through a massive pile of garbage in Karachi. 'In Pakistan', he said, 'poor folks depend on garbage for their daily bread.'

For Roxanne, it was when she was growing up on the Caribbean island of Jamaica. She recalls her aunt throwing banana peels and eggshells into one area for use in feeding their livestock.

For Sam, it was visiting family in Egypt as a four-year-old and seeing people burning garbage in the street. The smell overwhelmed him, and he remembers thinking, 'Wow, garbage in America just disappears.'

When did you first become aware of trash? Ask yourself that question, then turn to someone you know and ask them the same question. Share how your parents educated you about trash—share the good, the bad, and how that perspective has changed.

Trash Comes from What We Consume

Overconsuming can blind us to our role as stewards of the Earth—what in Islam we call being the *khalifah*. Being protectors of the planet means checking our consumption habits. We consume things every day—by eating, drinking, cleaning, travelling, buying new possessions, and by using the planet's resources in a multitude of ways. Far too often our constant consumption creates constant waste. Rising mounds of trash result in increased toxicity in the land, the air, the oceans and riverways, and also in our bodies. After all, we are all part of the Oneness of God and His creation (*tawhid*), the first principle of a Green Deen, so what we do to the planet is a reflection of what we are doing to ourselves.

But what is our role as stewards of the Earth? Some believe our covenant with God (*amanah*) means we are Earth's superior beings and that we therefore have the right to do what we want with the Earth—to extract what we want from it, to use it as we desire without regard for the effect of our consumption on the planet and the rest of its beings. Under this belief, industries pull fossil fuels out of the ground and destroy mountaintops to extract coal—with devastating effects on the natural ecology of these areas.

Others believe that *amanah* means we are responsible for taking care of the planet, safeguarding it, and seeing it as 'on loan' from our Creator. They believe that we have been given this brief moment on Earth and that we should leave the

Earth better than we found it. Islam advances the latter belief. In the Qur'an, Allah tells Muslims that He blessed humanity with the natural world:

> It is Allah who has created the heavens and the earth and sends down rain from the skies, and with it brings out fruits wherewith to feed you; and the rivers (also) has he made subject to you. And He has made subject to you the sun and the moon, both diligently following their courses; and the Night and the Day has He (also) made subject to you. (Qur'an 14:32–33)

I reflect on these signs (*ayat*) and realise how the seas, the rivers, the sun, and the moon do in fact serve us every day. They quench our thirst, they allow us to travel; they give us heat and light, time to sleep, and time to work. But Allah also advises:

> And He gives you of all that you ask for. But if you count the favours of Allah, never will you be able to number them. (Qur'an 14:34)

This *ayah* suggests that our understanding of natural resources as limited may be false. Perhaps what's limited is our understanding of how best to use these resources—not wasting them by overconsumption, not polluting them with the by-products of our overconsumption, but rather living in balance with nature (*mizan*) so as to sustain Earth's resources for all time. We have to change the narrative from one of scarcity to one that emphasizes that we have all we need, and that the story is about what can we do to make sure what natural resources are available are there for the present and far into the future.

The Prophet Muhammad (peace be upon him) said, 'The

world is beautiful and verdant, and verily God, be He exalted, has made you His stewards in it, and He sees how you acquit yourselves.'[1] The idea here is that as stewards, we will be judged according to our actions—according to whether we maintain or destroy the beauty of the Earth.

Greening Your Deen Is a Political, Economic, and Religious Imperative

As we green our everyday consumption practises, we also need to consider the political, economic, and religious dimensions of our use of the planet's resources. Here in America, we live under the guided political and economic systems of democracy and free-market capitalism. Although these systems have provided us with an amazing standard of living, they have in some ways proved inadequate for the task now before us as stewards of the Earth. In this century, it falls to us to understand the limitations of these systems so we can be open to and embrace broader and more inclusive systems that respect the Oneness of all creation (*tawhid*). In learning how to be true stewards of the Earth, we must commit to making our political and economic systems work better in defence of the planet.

The politics of consumption are the assumptions about how power and status affect what we consume. For example, one assumption of consumption is that it provides the fuel for development, financial prowess, and economic gain and is therefore politically appropriate. Another assumption is that consumption can assault the natural world and is therefore politically inappropriate.

Our attitudes about consumption are often affected by

the politics of consumption, depending on where we stand. Is consumption allowing us a better life, more liberty, and the pursuit of happiness? Or is consumption causing us to work long hours without enough pay? What remains uncontested is that our current attitudes about consumption are resulting in overconsumption—which is wreaking havoc on the planet.

The call to protect our planet comes from both the political right and the political left. Democrat Al Gore's *Earth in the Balance* and Republican Newt Gingrich's *A Contract with the Earth* each seeks to show us the harmful consequences of our consumptive actions. Both agree that we have to do something to protect the planet.

Our patterns of consumption and overconsumption have done the planet great injustice. Islam, like all religions, commands us to move toward what is just (*adl*) and away from what is unjust. Moving toward justice requires understanding the Earth's delicate balance (*mizan*)—a balance created by God but entrusted to us (*amanah*). This balance is purposeful.

Allah says in the Qur'an:

> We created not the heavens, the earth, and all between them merely in (idle) sport. We created them not except for just ends. (Qur'an 44:38–39)

Overconsumption on a broad scale—manifesting as overfishing, factory farming, and growth by any means necessary—has led to depleted oceans, nutritionless food, and nonstop expansion of development and markets, all unbalancing the Earth.

Overconsumption also steers us away from the Islamic principle of the Oneness of Allah and His creation (*tawhid*). The Prophet Muhammad (peace be upon him) reminded humanity that the Oneness of creation means that benefit for one is benefit for all, saying, 'There is a reward in doing good to every living thing.'[2] Similarly, harming one thing is like harming everything.

We are quite used to taking from the bounty God has provided—we take this bounty for granted, and contemporary marketing tells us that our value as human beings will increase if we reach for items of high economic value. As a consequence, we use so many things not because they bring any real or tangible benefit to our lives, but rather because they make us feel relevant.[3]

Capitalism—and for that matter, socialism, and all other economic or human-derived systems of organisation and government—also disconnect humans from the natural world. These systems reduce us to units of production—we become relevant only by what we can create.

In contrast, Islam teaches that we come with intrinsic value: We do not need to produce or acquire anything to be valuable. We are innately valuable, from birth to death. We all have a noble beginning and a noble end. Our soul has value because it is made by God. And when we recognise our own value and nurture the relationship we have with the Creator, we can begin to take better care of ourselves and see ourselves as a beautiful part of creation. We are also a sign (*ayah*) of Allah, and as one of his beautiful creations, we do not need to consume or create to have worth. Our worth is that Allah has made us. This is the spiritual antidote to the big lie of consumption: that we need things to create or consume to be relevant.

The by-product of a deeper understanding of oneself is consuming less and gaining a better environment to connect with other humans, the natural world, and Allah. Consuming less, even though you might have the means to consume a great deal, is a choice that should enable deeper relationships with the people you are close to. It is a choice that will allow you time to get your hands in dirt, start a garden, or walk more often, and consuming less is a choice that can lead you to have increased time and more focus when you go to worship God.

The unfortunate by-products of overconsumption and overproduction are pollution and climate change. The Qur'an recognises the human element in these consequences:

> Corruption has appeared on the land and in the sea because of what the hands of humans have wrought. This is in order that we give them a taste of the consequences of their misdeeds that perhaps they will turn to the path of right guidance. (Qur'an 30:41)

Many Islamic scholars concerned about the environment have cited this particular *ayah,* relating 'corruption' to pollution. Landfills are filling up with garbage and discarded goods.[4] Our overconsumption of fossil fuels is releasing great amounts of carbon dioxide into the atmosphere, greatly increasing the 'greenhouse gases' that trap heat in the atmosphere, resulting in the surface warming of the planet and oceans.

If we were to adopt policies that maintain economic growth but also reduce carbon emissions and the waste we create, we'd be praising God and protecting the planet. Humans are part of the problem, and we must be part of the solution.

In the Holy Qur'an, this last point is clear:

> But waste not by excess, for Allah loves not the wasters. (Qur'an 7:31)

We have been blessed by God with a bountiful planet that can suffice for all we need. One day we will be held accountable for how we have managed it and ourselves. A system based on waste and excess has turned us from stewards to dominators. This has resulted in oppressive systems and institutions across the world that have subjugated and exploited people. This oppression has left people emotionally damaged—and this damage is being used to promote consumption. People find solace in material goods. They buy things to feel better about themselves or to prove something about themselves. Instead of improving relationships with fellow humans, people create relationships with things that money can buy.

At its core, Islam is about developing a relationship with God. Islam then promotes relationship between people—families, neighbours, anyone. By putting at the forefront relationship-building between other people, Islam tries to help humans heal from the oppressions they have suffered and deemphasises materialism. Ultimately, just as we do not need to create to be relevant, nor do we need to consume to be relevant. Islam brings us into a state of balance (*mizan*) so that we can come to see the role of steward (*khalifah*) as part of a more mindful practise—a practise in which we see our time on Earth as an opportunity to leave the planet better than we found it.

Ask yourself this question: Has there ever been a time when you measured your own value by what you bought or consumed?

Chapter 2

The Environmental Movement as a Response to Overconsumption

What we think of as the environmental movement today has in reality been a longer process existing in three main phases. The first phase dealt primarily with the regulation of toxic substances that are a by-product of overconsumption. The second dealt with organising people to respond to the negative effects of pollution in marginalised communities. The third phase, where we are now, consists of transforming our lifestyles, seizing opportunities for innovation, and involving people in the movement who have never been involved before. There was also an important precursor to these three phases — the transformation of the management of resources after the worldwide colonial era.

Throughout each stage, Islam and the environmental movement have had much in common. Each phase contains elements that reflect the six principles of a Green Deen: understanding the Oneness of God and his creation (*tawhid*); seeing signs of God everywhere (*ayat*); being a steward of the Earth (*khalifah*); honouring the trust we have with God (*amanah*) to be protectors of the planet; moving toward justice (*adl*); and living in balance with nature (*mizan*). From the perspective of these principles, the environmental movement can be seen as an attempt to restore balance and justice to the Earth after the environmental destruction caused by overconsumption.

As you read this chapter, think about your own personal history. Where are your parents from? Your grandparents? How does your family history align with the stages and events of the environmental movement?

Colonial and Postcolonial Management of Natural Resources

To give a broader historical context to today's environmental movement, we need to look at the management of natural resources under eighteenth- and nineteenth-century colonialism and at a precursor to today's movement—the postcolonial transformation of resource management in the colonised nations. Colonialism, starting in the 1700s, was the process by which European nations took over (by their standards) less developed countries, giving Europeans access to the plentiful natural resources found around the world. These colonising nations used these resources to produce goods that created profits and also waste. In stripping these countries of their resources, the colonisers also created oppressive social orders that subjugated millions.[1]

Soon enough, by the 1900s, popular resistance movements began and eventually, by mid-century, achieved success against the colonial powers, who through the resources of their colonised peoples, industrialisation, and free-market capitalism had created the way of life that dominates the world today.

Over time, the will of the people of these countries to move toward justice (*adl*) in their own lands was too strong. One by one, former colonies liberated themselves politically and regained control over their natural resources. Unfortunately, some former colonies did not know how to manage their resources and therefore stayed indebted to the corporate structures of the colonial powers—for instance, to diamond companies in Sierra Leone, to fruit companies in Latin America, and to oil companies in Iraq.[2]

In the postcolonial period, formerly colonised nations began the long process of restoring justice to the management of their own natural resources, a process that continues through to the present day. They were, in effect, striving for justice within a Green Deen.

Since the beginning of the labour movement in the late 1800s, this search for justice was also trapped in an ideological struggle that is the opposite of a Green Deen. On one side were democracy and free-market capitalism; on the other, Marxist socialism. Each of these Western ideas was heralded as the right idea of social organisation. Muslim nations were trapped in the chess game of the post–World War II Cold War, which provided the staging grounds for this conflict of ideas. Afghanistan famously struggled with British and Soviet influence, the result of which tore at the fabric of civil society, stunting its development. Almost all of the emergent African nations—in particular, Egypt, Algeria, and Somalia—were involved in this dichotomy of communism versus capitalism.

At the core, neither is a choice in the Deen, or religion, of Islam. Libya, a Muslim nation, struck another chord by calling for another path of pan-Africanism, a plan to unite all the African nations. Still, the stage was set for a battle over power and control in a postcolonial world that was splitting roughly between capitalist and socialist thought. To understand how both systems are inconsistent with a Green Deen, let's look at their essential elements. Democracy allows the participation of all citizens. Free-market capitalism offers big rewards to anyone with the ambition and the opportunity to produce marketable goods. The basic organising principle of democratic capitalism is the individual. In contrast, the basic organising principle of Marxist socialism is a guided economy centred around the needs of the group.

A Green Deen is neither socialist nor capitalist — it is interested in both the individual and the collective.[3] Capitalism and socialism see humans as units of production and consumption. Islam sees each individual human being as having intrinsic value and worth. Your soul is what makes you special, not what you make or use. You are not just a cog in a capitalist or socialist machine. At the same time, you have a responsibility to the people, the plants, the animals, the air, the water, and the land around you. When we are living a Green Deen, we recognise that we rely on all of creation for our survival, and that all of creation relies on us for its survival. Once again, we are all connected to the Earth, and the Earth is connected back to us — the principle of Oneness (*tawhid*).

The model of democratic capitalism offered by the United States prevailed in the twentieth century but was not without flaws. For example, racism, with roots in the colonial infrastructure, reinforced structural inequalities. These included systemic ways in which inequality was imposed, be it through lack of opportunity to education or through infrastructure control, such as limited resources, redlining to disallow for home ownership by certain groups, or policies that institutionalised Jim Crow laws in the South. Structural inequalities created a lack of equal opportunity for blacks, Native Americans, and immigrants before they assimilated.[4] Internally, some of these inconsistencies have been addressed through the civil rights movement, and, externally, the United States has made some effort to reform its relationship with former colonies.

In a speech delivered in Cairo on 4 June 2009, President Barack Obama referred to the effects of colonialism and the Cold War on the relationship between Muslim nations and the West, saying: 'Tension has been fed by colonialism that denied rights and opportunities to many Muslims, and a Cold War in which Muslim-majority countries were too often treated as proxies without regard to their own aspirations.'[5] These struggles, in places with large Muslim populations, such as India, Nigeria, and Indonesia, were part of a dynamic that has affected the Muslim world and the way it exists today, politically, economically, socially, and environmentally.

Indonesia

Indonesia provides us with an example of a colonised nation that underwent centuries of colonial exploitation of its resources, finally gained its independence and control over its resources in the twentieth century, then slowly developed into a green nation.

The first Europeans to arrive in Indonesia were the Portuguese in 1512, followed by British and Dutch traders, all of whom sought control of the country's resources, especially its spices. In 1602, the Dutch established the Dutch East India Company, which dominated Indonesian resources until its bankruptcy in 1800, after which the Netherlands established the Dutch East Indies as a nationalised colony.

The Dutch left in 1940 during World War II, spurred by the invasion of the Japanese. The transfer of power sparked an Indonesian independence movement led by Sukarno, and the nation claimed independence in 1945.

Soon after, Indonesia grappled with democracy, authoritarianism, and communism. The military leader, Suharto, took power in 1965 and led Indonesia into the era of foreign investments—basically, modern-day colonialism. In 1998, Suharto resigned, and since then, Indonesia has been attempting to strengthen itself as a democracy, holding its first presidential election in 2004.[6]

With control over its own resources, rapid industrialisation, and a large population (206 million, almost 90 percent of whom are Muslim), Indonesia has suffered from its own share of environmental issues, including widespread pollution of its waterways, soil, and air, and destruction of its forests and wildlife by industries such as mining, timber, and manufacturing.[7] It has therefore recently made a special effort to address environmental issues. Indonesia has one of the few eco-mosques in the world and has developed green infrastructure development through funding of clean energy technology.[8] There is even a Green Building Council, which recently issued green building rating tools.[9]

One of the tragedies of modern times is that when former colonies liberated themselves from political control, that control was supplanted by the economic control of large corporations. I describe this phase as a precursor of the environmental movement because, while in its essence the postcolonial phase was about the management of natural resources and control over land use policies, it was not couched as such. Former colonies wanted political power to determine how they would control their own resources, yet they, by and large, had bought into the pervading notion that development, the Western way, was the only way forward.

What remains are the consequences of this postcolonial era. We see how corporate interests are trying to take resources from places such as the African Muslim nations mentioned earlier, which are still locked in a struggle to control their own respective environments. This ongoing struggle, whether it be through legislation in Indonesia or direct action in Nigeria's Niger Delta, is part of our Deen, the path or religion of Islam, that we need to understand as we move toward justice (*adl*) in the way that human beings interact with the land, the air, the sea, and importantly—one another.

Conservation as Part of a Green Deen

Beginning roughly in the late 1800s, the conservation movement was a by-product of the industrial age in reaction to overdevelopment, which had negatively affected the balance that God made in nature. This overdevelopment was fuelled by overconsumption. Forests were cut down and rivers polluted. Coal-fired factories and trains stitching across industrial towns spewed ash and soot into the streets. Growth and development happened so quickly that it soon strangled the natural world. In response, large industrial cities, not immune to the negative effects of development, started to make conservation a priority.[10]

The conservation movement had big personalities and big champions. One was President Theodore Roosevelt, who said, 'I recognise the right and duty of this generation to develop and use the natural resources of our land; but I do not recognize the right to waste them, or to rob, by wasteful use, the generations that come after us.'[11] Roosevelt realised the injustice that occurs when people are wasteful, and his words echo balance (*mizan*) and justice (*adl*), two of the six basic Islamic principles necessary to follow in living a Green Deen. Another early champion of conservation was the poet Walt Whitman, who was instrumental in getting parks into urban areas that were choked by filth from overdevelopment.[12] Conservation efforts are responsible for the creation of parks and preserves all over the world and have helped to preserve natural areas from deforestation, logging, and the interests of developers.[13]

Still, while conservation efforts were good, creating national parks and protecting specific areas from developers did not do enough to restore the natural world's divine balance. Conservation is not enough in a Green Deen. Yes, we need to conserve the natural world so that it can be allowed to maintain its balance, but we need also to think in terms of managing the resources that are of so much value so that we can benefit from the bounty of the planet. A Green Deen is about using the resources of the Earth smartly and efficiently.

Environmental Regulation and Protection

The next phase of the environmental movement focused on the unjust actions of polluting industries. After the world was trapped in wars over ideas and resources (World Wars I and II, and the wars for independence in colonial countries), the results of this rapid industrialisation—and its negative consequences—became apparent. Beginning roughly in the mid-1900s, governments began to require regulation of industries and to mandate the protection of wildlife and open space. Typically, a company would manufacture a product. The manufacturing process would create waste and pollute air, water, and land. The pollution would continue for decades, and people would get sick—really sick. The company would try to cover up pollution and illness. Eventually, a courageous person or group of people would step up and demand regulation of the company. The demand for regulation would first become policy, then regulatory guidelines for all companies in the same industry would appear.[14]

The 1970 Clean Air Act was one regulatory outcome of this product-pollution-illness-advocacy trajectory. In 1948, the small village of Donora, Pennsylvania, home to American Steel and Wire and Donora Zinc Works, was blanketed by a thick smog caused by air pollution from the factories. Seventy people died. Advocates lobbied for regulation, which resulted in the 1955 Air Pollution Control Act. As time progressed, air pollution came from more than just factories—cars became a major culprit. The 1970 Clean Air Act included emissions standards for automobiles and gave citizens the right to take legal action against entities in violation of these standards.[15]

People began to understand that the systems of water, air, and soil were all connected and that pollution in one would lead to pollution to another. In 1962, Rachel Carson's landmark book *Silent Spring* opened our eyes to the dangerous effects of pesticides on our water and soil systems. These dangers to the natural world would eventually turn into dangers for humans. Ten years later, use of the pesticide DDT was banned in the United States. While people were not explicitly talking about seeing the signs of God in nature and observing what we were doing to the planet, Rachel Carson's spirit was essentially causing millions to see the Earth as sacred.

Muslims were part of the process of raising awareness of the Earth as sacred as early as 1966, when the young scholar and Iranian Muslim philosopher Seyyed Hossein Nasr delivered a series of lectures at the University of Chicago in which he examined the relationship between man and nature. Nasr became the father of the modern Muslim environmental movement, and these lectures were later published as *Man and Nature: The Spiritual Crisis of Modern Man.*[16]

In 1970, the U.S. Environmental Protection Agency (EPA) was formed, with a mission to foster conditions under which man and nature can live in productive harmony. The EPA would from then on be responsible for creating and enforcing regulations on industries and citizens in order to protect the planet. Regulations picked up momentum in the 1970s. The Water Pollution Control Act of 1972 regulated pollution coming from industrial facilities, and the Resource Conservation and Recovery Act of 1976 (RCRA) set national goals for protecting human health, conserving energy, reducing the generation of waste, and ensuring that wastes are managed in an environmentally sound manner.[17]

Environmental Justice—People's Environmentalism

The environmental justice movement came about as a response to the disconnection between people and planet. Islam has a lot to say about this disconnection. In the environmental justice movement, trees, animals, and humans all have the same level of importance.[18] They are all significant

parts of the ecosystem. This part of the environmental justice movement essentially follows the principles of a Green
Deen—it believes that human beings and the planet are One
(*tawhid*) and that justice (*adl*) to the environment—including
animals and trees—means justice to people as well. Similarly,
injustice to the environment means injustice to people. For
example, as pollution increases, health decreases.

However, government regulations did not accomplish effective community organising. As environmentalists Michael
Shellenberger and Ted Nordhaus wrote in their 2004 essay
'The Death of Environmentalism: Global-Warming Politics
in a Post-Environmental World': 'Our parents and elders ex-
perienced something during the 1960s and 70s that today
seems like a dream: the passage of a series of powerful environmental laws too numerous to list, from the Endangered
Species Act to Clean Water acts to the National Environmental Policy Act.'[19] However, people realised that more than
policy was necessary for balance between people and planet.
Shellenberger and Nordhaus continue: 'It was also then, at
the height of the movement's success, that the seeds of failure were planted. . . Success created a strong confidence and in
some cases, bald arrogance that the environmental protection
frame was enough to succeed at a policy levels.'[20]

The Green Economy Movement

The final phase of the environmental movement is where we
are now—finding economic opportunity in the environmental movement. In 2005, the murmurs of the green economy
were already beginning to make noise. Activists like Van
Jones, then of the Ella Baker Center (Oakland, California),
and Majora Cater of Sustainable South Bronx (New York

City) were eyeing the opportunity that could come in the environmental movement to support the communities they were already working in.

The green economy really changes the way we determine accountability. If rooted in environmental justice, it responds to a question I asked in 2005: 'Who's going to benefit from the new green industry? Will the hierarchy stay the same when the change comes?'[21]

Who will benefit? The real question is: Who will put in the effort? The critique of the green economy phase is that it is a market solution to something the free market created. That what it encourages is more consumption. That it does not address the root cause—that overconsumption got us into this ecological mess. The promise of the green economy is that it can encourage innovation and efficiency and increase pollination of ideas and collaboration across sectors.

Which sectors? This approach places accountability not only with governments, to provide regulation, but also with everyday people—to make new choices and decisions with their dollar to assign a collective value to products and services. It holds companies accountable to diversify their business models to incorporate the effect of their processes on the natural world and—with the laws of supply and demand—to respond to the demands of their consumers who hold Green Deen principles dear.

This 'people's environmentalism' approach has been described by Van Jones as a green growth alliance,[22] and it includes the 'civic sector'—shorthand for non-profits and religious institutions. Allah has made us all stewards of the Earth, and our collective opportunity for action has come in the green economy movement, guided by the principles of environmental justice, which place humans as part of the natural world. All sectors now have an opportunity to be held accountable for the ecological crisis—and also to score a net gain from the cleanup and transition to a greener, cleaner, more equitable future that affirms the Oneness of God and His creation. We see the opportunity in His signs (*ayat*) in nature. We are moved toward justice (*adl*) economically and environmentally to ensure the balance (*mizan*)—all to be the best stewards (*khalifah*) we can be, to honor the trust or covenant (*amanah*) we have with our Creator to leave the Earth better than we found it.

The next chapter, 'Green Muslims', highlights Muslims who are actively involved in the environmental movement—from conservation, protection, and regulation to fighting for environmental justice and finding opportunity in the green economy. We are already active in the transformation of our current relationship with the Earth into being stewards of the Earth. No finger wagging here to tell you to starting thinking about it. The people whose stories we share in 'Green Muslims' have already committed and invested time into their Green Deen.

Of course, this transformation requires work, and the Prophet Muhammad (peace be upon him) provided the best example for being a steward of the Earth. When Aishah, the wife of the Holy Prophet (peace be upon her), was asked, 'What was the usual practice of the Messenger of God at home?' she replied, 'He was a human from among other humans, he himself removed the lice from his clothing, milked his goats, and did all his work himself.'[23]

What work are you willing to do to green your Deen?

Chapter 3

Green Muslims

I was inspired to write this book after reflecting on my own Green Deen and meeting other Green Muslims who are living the six principles of a Green Deen. I sought out Muslims who are committed to being stewards of the Earth (*khalifah*), who understand the Oneness of God and His creation (*tawhid*), who look for signs of Allah (*ayat*) in everything around them, who move toward justice (*adl*), who seek to protect the delicate balance of the natural world (*mizan*), and who honour our sacred trust with God to protect the planet (*amanah*). Happily, what I discovered is that Muslims are involved in every aspect of the stewardship of the Earth.

Stewardship of the Earth comes in many forms. Green Muslims like Aziz Siddiqi of Houston, Texas, are actively involved in environmental policy. Others, like Sarah Sayeed of the Bronx, New York City, are Green Muslims who ensure environmental justice by working with the interfaith environmental community. While this whole book reflects the active involvement of Muslims in the environmental movement, this chapter focuses on some distinct and inspirational efforts, including the famous DC Green Muslims in our nation's capital.

The Colour Green

Muslims have a personal connection to the colour green. Colour is a refraction of light. In Islam, light is the substance of creation. Somewhere, in the farthest reaches of the universe, Allah is creating from pure light. Green is an aspect of that light and is reflected all over the world. The favorite colour of the Prophet Muhammad (peace be upon him) was green: 'Among the colours, green was liked the most, as it is the colour of the clothing in Jannah (paradise).'[1]

Allah paints his *ayat*s (signs of nature) in a tapestry of green all over the world. He does so from the lushness of Muir Woods in northern California to the evergreens and ferns of the East as they welcome the flowers after spring rains. Green is the colour of the Waipio Valley in the heart of the Big Island, Hawaii. In this valley, you can dip, drink, and make ablution (*wudu*) in freshwater streams surrounded by green. Green are the mountainous ridges of the Rockies, covered with ferns that host the snow in winter. Green is the colour of life on all corners of the planet. And, yes, people can be green too.

Are You a Green Muslim?

Your own family might be the best place to look for signs of a Green Deen in action. That's certainly where I look first. I come from a family in which our father taught us that the Earth is a mosque. My father spends much time in the outdoors being absorbed by the natural world. Connecting to nature is how my father connects with God.

One morning while writing this book, I received the following e-mail from my dad. He had just arrived at a remote section of Maine for one of his customary sojourns into the natural world. His goal was to be immersed in the signs of Allah and to pray and worship the Creator while surrounded by those signs, free from distraction.

> Alhamdullilah [All Praise Due to Allah], I arrived in Maine safely. Tonite I am spending the night at Sebago Lake (car camping). Tomorrow I will be traveling north along the coast to the ocean. Not sure how many nights I will spend there. Will figure that out when I get there. I am expecting Wednesday to be a rainy day, but although it's partially cloudy, the weather is nice. Sebago Lake is a huge lake—I even heard they have a navy SEALs training base somewhere near here. I probably won't get a chance to e-mail after today, so I'll check in again Thursday, Insha'Allah [God Willing]. Make Dua [supplication] for me, I will do the same for you.

Daddy (yes, I still call him that) sent that message to all six of us children. He is the best man I have ever known. Of course I know he is not perfect, but he is still my father. He has always done his best to guide and protect me. I cannot say that I have never disappointed him, but I have never raised my voice to him. I am his son through and through, and I love what he loves as much as I love him. Trying to be a steward of the Earth is one way I am following in his footsteps.

We are a proud people rooted in the land. My father's family comes from Virginia, where my grandmother was one of nine in a traditionally well-educated churchgoing black family. Back in Scottsburg, Virginia, you can still see the grave markers from my extended family going back to the 1860s. My father's father, my grandfather, was born on a Native American reservation in upstate New York in 1908.

My father is a man of firm principle. He chose the path of Islam and made his life's motto 'There is no God but Allah and Muhammad is His Messenger.' This is the declaration of faith in Islam, the one thing a person must say and believe to be considered Muslim. Like my dad, I am a Muslim. As a child of converts to Islam, I did wonder if my parents' Islamic path was the right path for me. I spent a long time pondering this question. I became aware of other systems of thought, belief, and practise. I believed that humans could not have created and developed this world alone. I was not an atheist—I believed in an omnipotent Creator. Eventually I decided that Islam was the best method for decision making I could find, that it was what I wanted to guide me in my life and the religion I wanted to raise my children in one day.

My dedication to the environment, my commitment to being green, starts with my father and stays alive by my Islam. I try my best to not separate what I do and how I live from what I eat. I try my best to treat the planet as sacred, like the mosque I believe it is. Finally, I try to better my Green Deen by learning from others who choose to root their love of the planet in their faith.

The Pioneer

Aziz Siddiqi is a Green Muslim who has been on the forefront of environmental policy since the 1970s.[2] I will refer to Mr. Siddiqi here as Uncle Aziz, 'Uncle' being a term of respect in many cultures. He is a pioneer of sustainability who has been working to ensure that the air you breathe is properly protected and regulated. It was his orientation as a Muslim that gave him the perspective to focus on the basic principles of balance (*mizan*) and Oneness (*tawhid*), which helped him become one of the most important figures in the history of the environmental movement.

In the late 1960s, Uncle Aziz was a young doctoral candidate doing groundbreaking research in chemical engineering. His work was noticed by an official from the University of Houston, and a few years later, upon completing his studies, he was immediately offered a job there. Soon he found himself guiding the development of a curriculum that would help the U.S. Environmental Protection Agency (EPA) carry out its new mission of enforcing the Clean Air Act.

In 1973 the EPA was only three years old and did not understand the full breadth of its power. The EPA, its scientists, and its partner agencies needed to be trained on how to monitor pollution from chimneys and other commonly used industrial practices. Uncle Aziz had to learn how to explain his research in chemical engineering to this group of regulators. He also wrote the training materials used to teach EPA scientists how to sample ambient air and develop pollution controls.

Eventually, Uncle Aziz became a national authority and a local community leader. He lectured widely and wrote articles that became canon in the industry. His status as a well-respected scientist working to protect the planet was balanced with a reputation for being a pious member of the Muslim community of Houston. In time he used his contacts, expertise, passion, and background to start his own consulting firm, which he runs today.

Along with being credited with helping Houston significantly reduce its smog levels over the years, Uncle Aziz is the president and CEO of one of the largest Islamic institutions in the United States—the Islamic Society of Greater Houston. Under his leadership, the society is using its multimillion-dollar budget to buy land and develop mosques that include a community centre, a school, and a free clinic for the general public.

Uncle Aziz embodies the spirit of protecting the planet, protecting the Earth, and praising Allah. His mind never rests, for he is constantly innovating. Today, he is thinking about starting a new venture concerning energy efficiency and conservation.

Interfaith Green Muslims

Interfaith work is one of the best places to exercise a Green Deen. Most faith traditions believe that humans will be held accountable for their actions. Individual responsibility reflects the trust (*amanah*) we entered into with God when we were blessed with the gift of choice.

Allah says in the Qur'an:

That Day will Man be told (all) that he put forward, and all that he put back. (Qur'an 75:13)

'That Day' refers to the Day of Resurrection, and the rest points to humanity's actions while on Earth. The notion of a life after death is a strong organising principle for Muslims, Buddhists, Hindus, Christians, and Jews. Many people of faith are mindful of their actions as a way to ensure a peaceful and heavenly afterlife. It has been said that faith can speak the common language in the public square—a belief that speaks to the ability of people of faith to create something that everyone can be a part of.

Sarah Sayeed is a Green Muslim who lives in the Bronx, New York City.[3] Her neighbourhood has seen the best and worst of times in New York City's recent history, and Sarah is most committed to the Green Deen principle of justice (*adl*). Following this principle, she helps to organise people of all faiths for environmental justice.

Sarah works at the New York Interfaith Center, located on the Upper West Side of Manhattan adjacent to the Columbia University campus. The centre's unique nickname, 'the God Box', was coined when people of faith began moving their organisations into the building. As a Muslim activist working from the God Box, Sarah is connected to just about every relevant Muslim leader in New York City. She understands the nuance of secular and religious culture, is well educated, and loves New York. To Sarah, New York City is a mosque.

Sarah is one of the core organisers of the Faith Leaders for Environmental Justice, a gathering of faith leaders—Buddhist, Jewish, Christian, and Muslim—who are deeply concerned about the environment, particularly climate change and food security. Over the past three years, these leaders have come together on a regular basis to cultivate a common language of stewardship (*khalifah*). According to Sarah, stewardship of the Earth can compel people of faith to engage in interfaith work without having to agree on basic 'creed'.

The Faith Leaders share information on pressing issues of food scarcity, solid waste management, energy use, and green jobs. On Earth Day 2010, they launched their 'green map', which identifies locations throughout Harlem offering access

to healthy food to people trapped in New York City food deserts—areas without access to fresh foods.

Interfaith work can offer a clear message to policy makers
about the moral imperative. 'Politicians', says Sarah, 'need to
hear the moral reasoning to remind people of the moral need
to act in a just way beyond what they would normally do.' Lisa
Sharon Harper, founder of New York Faith and Justice and
one of Sarah's co-conveners says, 'The faith voice gives gravity
to the numbers.'[4] The lesson to policy makers is the same—
overcoming any challenge requires coalition building.

Sarah once told me that all spiritual paths tread upon the
Earth. I had the honour of watching many of these paths converge at an interfaith Ramadan event in 2009, at which I mod-
erated a panel on pollution with a Jewish scholar, a Christian
educator, a Jain activist, and a Muslim imam.[5] Muhammad
Hatim of New Jersey used the words *mischief* and *corruption*
synonymously with *pollution*. 'Are humans here to pollute?' he
asked. 'Are they here to cause corruption and mischief? Are
we responsible for the state that the planet is in ecologically?
What are the signs that can tell us how we are to live on our
only planet?'[6] Those questions struck me primarily because
I realised that each faith had faith-specific answers to those
questions. Each panellist went on to describe what they felt
were their responsibilities to the planet. I reflected on Islam
and recalled the verse of the Qur'an that says:

> *lakum deenukum wa li al-deen:* 'to you then be your way and to
> me mine.' (Qur'an 109:6)

All of the Deens—the different spiritual paths—that
day at the interfaith event recognised their coexistence on

the planet. They each made an unwavering commitment to restoring justice to the Earth.

The DC Green Muslims

The Washington, DC, Metro area has become a hub of Green Deen activity.[7] The ADAMS (All Dulles Area Muslim Society) Center Mosque is home to the DC Green Muslims, a loosely organised group of like-minded Muslims interested in stopping the detrimental effects of climate change. They exemplify the principles of justice (*adl*) and trust (*amanah*) and are committed to both personal adaptation and collective responsibility. They are a politically active community and truly see the DC Metro area as a mosque. The centre has also just published its *ADAMS Center Green Environment Guide.*[8]

The DC Green Muslims foster fellowship, and my first interaction with them was at one of their famous dinners, held in a building that was once an opulent home but which is now owned by the DC Parks Department. This particular dinner was a networking event for young professionals—a way for Muslims to connect to the larger green movement, to be engaged in the political process, and to be involved in something that affirms and strengthens their Deen. My sister Tauhirah, who works on water quality issues, and I drove down together from New York to attend the dinner. (I'll be discussing Tauhirah's work further in part III of this book.) I learned that the group's first Ramadan Iftar—the breaking of the Ramadan fast—consisted of only fifteen people. Their first conversations were on a broad scale, dealing with larger concepts and the intersections between Islam and the environment. That small group had grown to the event I attended, which hosted more than two hundred people, and the discussions there focused on tangible steps these young leaders could take to encourage their broader community to build a Green Muslim movement.

The DC Green Muslims have participated in local greening efforts alongside non-Muslim environmental organisations. For example, they collaborated with the DC Parks and People to plant trees and clean up a local park. Sarah Jawaid, a DC Green Muslim and a key DC Green Muslim organiser, says, 'We are trying to bridge the gap between the young working professionals of the DC Green Muslims and local residents who face social and ecological injustices.'[9] They learned the importance of coalition building and the difficulty of sustained and consistent involvement partly because of the culture of DC itself—a transient city in which young people and politicos come and go. As interest in the dinners themselves was high and there was a core leadership, a shift occurred when those core leaders moved into other phases of their lives. There was a lull in participation until the efforts of a new crop of DC Green Muslims, led by Sarah Jawaid, came along.

Sarah got the DC Muslims to participate in the *Huffington Post*'s No Impact Week. This project gave people the opportunity to examine and reduce their ecological footprint by taking part in a short, intense period of conscious consumption supported by local and online communities. To make No Impact Week relevant to her fellow Muslims, Sarah created an addendum using Qur'anic references to highlight the ecospiritual ethics in Islam. 'As a result of this initiative', she says, 'we renewed a sense of community and reinvigorated our efforts to continue creating a space for Muslims to discuss environmental issues guided by spirituality.' The following chapters will continue to highlight the stories of Muslims who are significantly involved in the environmental movement and who have dedicated themselves to living a Green Deen. Each person exemplifies one or more of the Green Deen principles and contributes to the movement on an individual, family, and community level.

If you already consider yourself green, can you bring people together to create a sense of fellowship and tighten the bonds of your community around our shared trust (*amanah*) with Allah to protect the planet?

Chapter 4

Green Mosques

The mosque is the centre of religious and community life for Muslims. Around the globe, the mosque is primarily where people go to pray, but mosques also serve other functions as well. They are used as community centres where Muslims get married, gather after the sun sets in the holy month of Ramadan to end the daily fasting with a communal meal, and hold classes for youth—what some might call 'Sunday school'. Given the centrality of the mosque in Muslim life, it is the perfect place to start promoting a Green Deen.

Remember, living a Green Deen means opening your heart to the possibility of understanding the Oneness of God and His creation (*tawhid*); seeing the signs of God (*ayat*) everywhere; being a steward of the Earth (*khalifah*); honouring the trust we have from God to be a protector of the planet (*amanah*); moving toward justice (*adl*); and living in balance with nature (*mizan*).

Buildings, Energy, and Carbon Footprints

A Green Deen starts with the greening of your local mosque. Mosques are buildings, and buildings are where we use the most energy and emit the most greenhouse gases. According to the U.S. Department of Energy, buildings use 39 percent of the energy and 74 percent of the electricity consumed each year in the United States.[1] In New York City alone, buildings are responsible for nearly 80 percent of the city's 'carbon footprint', or its total amount of greenhouse gas emissions.[2]

Greenhouse gases—atmospheric gases that absorb and emit heat, thus regulating the temperature of the Earth—have been increasing because of human activities.[3] We often speak of greenhouse gases in terms of 'carbon footprint' as a shorthand way of referring to the amount of carbon dioxide, or its equivalent of other greenhouse gases, emitted by an entity or activity. The consumption of electricity, heating, and hot water in buildings accounts for a large part of this greenhouse gas footprint, and it involves us all. Our individual carbon footprints are what make up the whole.

To green a building—in this case, a mosque—it's important to look at buildings holistically. We need to examine what we can do with the structure and air circulation, but we also need to explore what we can do with some simple behavioural changes to reduce waste of energy and goods. Finally, we need to set goals—and challenge others to do the same.

Considerations in Greening a Mosque

Muslims who think differently about waste can create a Green Mosque. To think about how we can 'green the mosque', the centre of religious and community life, let's consider three things.

First, we need to consider the actual building. Mosque

buildings fall into two categories: pre-existing structures and new builds. Pre-existing structures are converted buildings that Muslims cleverly repurpose as mosques. New builds are mosques built from the ground up.

Second, we need to consider the people who use the mosque. Muslims are a diverse people, not a monolith. According to data gathered by Gallup, Muslims are the most diverse religious community in the country in terms of socioeconomic status, race, education level, and levels of practise. A mosque must appeal to people who are at all stages of their lives, and its purpose should be to connect them to the Oneness of God and His creation (*tawhid*), binding them to Allah so that they can realise their own self-worth.

Third, we need to consider what we bring into the mosque. This includes our food and what we eat it on—such as paper plates, plastic, and the dreaded Polystyrene. Can we think differently about waste? Maybe all we need are good, solid examples.

The holy mosques in Mecca and Medina both recycle wastewater.[4] This recycled water is called grey water. These holiest of sites set an important precedent for sustainability. Millions of Muslims travel to these holy mosques each year to perform the Hajj, the major religious pilgrimage to Mecca, and Umrah, the 'lesser' pilgrimage, which occurs along the same routes as the Hajj, but at a different time of the year. The Hajj is the largest gathering of people on the planet for one purpose, and it takes place in the heat and desolation of the Arabian Desert. Managing resources in this environment is a challenge. A lesson that can be learned here is that the Saudi Arabian government, the caretakers of the holy mosques, issued a fatwa—a legally non-binding religious ruling—that allows for treated wastewater to be recycled for use in performing the obligatory ablution (*wudu*) before prayer.[5]

Providing places for ablution is a critical function of any mosque. (I'll talk about ablution more when I talk about water in part IV of this book.) By issuing a fatwa, the Saudi Arabian government has said that this method of waste management, wastewater recycling, is permissible and encouraged. If the most important mosques in the world can issue an edict that sets a precedent for rethinking how we manage critical systems, then mosques all over the world can be transformed, and we can all better honour the trust (*amanah*) we have with God.

Green Building Equals Green Mosque

For a mosque to find balance, its members must first consider its geographic location and the climatic conditions. A Green Mosque is one that strives for balance with the climate it's in. Everything in creation is made in balance, and balance (*mizan*) is one of the six principles of a Green Deen. This consideration can optimise a mosque's energy use and the overall comfort and health of the Muslims who go there to worship, eat, and spend time. In the interest of being aware of the signs of God (*ayat*) in the natural world, I'll consider four different types of climates here: temperate, hot and humid, hot and arid, and cold.

Temperate Climates

In a temperate climate, the main concern is balancing the inside and outside temperatures. Generally, in temperate climates, the climate can change dramatically over the course of a day.[6] A Green Mosque should therefore be equipped with an energy system that can be manually adjusted to reflect sudden changes. The sun's light should also be used in these environments—sunroofs are critical to keeping energy costs down and capturing the warmth of the sun. Proper insulation is also needed so that when the weather is cooler, as at night, the heating systems do not have to overwork to keep the temperature at a comfortable level.

Hot and Humid Climates

In a hot and humid climate, an efficient cooling system is the key to a Green Mosque. Many pre-existing buildings that have been repurposed into mosques tend to be stuffy and poorly ventilated. They rely upon expensive air-conditioning systems that use a lot of energy and create high electricity bills. The main concern in this kind of climate is keeping the humid air outside of the mosque. Maintaining a good ventilation system that pushes the humid air out and keeps the inside air dry will keep the mosque cool.

An excellent example of a Green Mosque in a state of balance with its hot and humid climate is the Manoa mosque on Hawaii's main island of Oahu.[7] This mosque is a large converted home in a residential neighbourhood. Upon entering, you are on a large deck, where you kick off your sandals. The sides of the mosque, where there would typically be windows, are large, removable panels. An awning above the deck keeps that area protected from the hot sun, and plants provide additional shade. The combination of exposure to the outside and protection from the sun creates a cross-flow of ventilation that results in humid air outside and dry air inside. Though the Manoa mosque does not boast an inner courtyard, such a courtyard can also help with ventilation in a hot and humid climate.

Hot and Dry Climates

In a hot and arid (dry) climate, such as the desert, a Green Mosque would be very simple, as exemplified by a small mosque at the top of Mount Sinai, on the Sinai Peninsula of Egypt.[8] It was on this mountain that Moses, a prophet in Islam, Judaism, and Christianity, received the Ten Commandments. Pilgrims of all faiths hike up the rocky steps to the historic mountaintop every day. There they find a mosque of about thirty square metres. It has no windows and is made of mud brick. In hot and dry climates, the main concern is dust. Therefore openings in building are limited and small, and walls are thick. This design also ensures that hot air from the outside does not come in during the day. At night, once the sun has set, cool air flows in and the temperature drops; when the sun rises, the heating process is slower, since the inside of the mosque is cool to begin with. A similar design is at work in the Islamic Center of Tucson, near the University of Arizona. It has few windows, and the doors and walls are made from heavy materials.[9]

Cold Climates

Maintaining a Green Mosque in a cold climate is a study in balancing temperature and money. First, the building must maintain a decent temperature internally so that worshippers are not freezing and uncomfortable. Second, this temperature must be maintained at a reasonable expense. The tension between temperature and cost is common to cold-weather mosques because mosques often rely upon donations from the congregation to pay for basic maintenance. Water, heating, and electricity are not cheap.

A Green Mosque in a cold climate is appropriately weatherised. The key to successful weatherisation is to test the building for inefficiency by conducting an energy audit. The expense for the audit will be made up in lower energy bills later. This test is especially important in pre-existing structures, to determine whether the mosque is wasting heat through small cracks and poor insulation. Remember that preexisting mosques are repurposed buildings.

Once the audit report is in, there are a variety of ways to weatherise a cold-climate mosque that will improve its energy efficiency. Insulating the outside walls with fireproof-treated recycled newspaper (as opposed to the much less effective fibreglass) will address major heat loss. Weather stripping around windows and doors and caulking to fill in cracks and crevices will help manage smaller heat leaks. Replacing or recommissioning boilers will improve air and exhaust systems. Finally, replacing old windows will help each of the other measures.

In building a new mosque from the ground up in cold climates, builders should follow LEED (Leadership in Energy and Environmental Design) green building standards. These standards are developed by the U.S. Green Building Council and help determine the efficiency of appliances and lighting systems and how to use renewable and clean energy sources. Building according to LEED standards will go a long way toward maintaining a balance between cold outside temperatures, the desire for indoor warmth, and the need for an affordable energy bill.

Greening Mosques Is a Global Movement

Around the world, the greening of mosques has become something of a movement. In the United Kingdom, the Islamic Foundation for Ecology and Environmental Sciences has coined the term *eco-mosques*. A group of students in Abu Dhabi have designed a mosque that taps no electricity from the grid. Instead, it uses solar panels, wind towers, geothermal cooling, shading devices, wind turbines, and natural ventilation.[10] The mosque in Singapore boasts a 'green wall' of climbing plants.[11] Another green mosque, the Al-Markaz al-Najmi mosque, has opened in Manchester, England, with some of the same features as the Abu Dhabi mosque, such as solar paneling, underfloor heating, and low-energy lightbulbs.[12]

All these techniques, adapted by mosques around the globe, can be included in a 'how to green a mosque' guide. In fact, this is an area in which much more work needs to be done. We know already about LEED standards, which use a rating system of points to give a designation of how 'green' a certain building is. Muslims could employ best practices from around the globe to develop a similar standard for mosques. Perhaps if you have a background in the environment, engineering, or construction, you can be a part of this effort. Developing a mosque LEED standard should fold in standard environmentally friendly building techniques as well as incorporate the principles of a Green Deen. Of course, the key is to start with education of the people in the mosques so that they are better stewards of the Earth.

Green Mosques Are Made by Stewards of the Earth

Now that we've considered the greening of a mosque by greening the actual building, let's consider the greening of a mosque in relation to the people who use it. Remember, one principle of a Green Deen is that human beings are stewards of the Earth (*khalifah*). To be stewards of a mosque means to transform our behaviour by letting go of some of the unsustainable behaviour patterns we have developed. In the spirit of providing for all our brothers and sisters, regardless of what social or economic status they are in, we need to organise our mosques so that the community moves collectively toward justice (*adl*) in their dealings with one another and the natural world. We can build mosques that train congregants to see themselves as part of the Oneness (*tawhid*) of Allah and His creation.[13]

A Green Mosque is one that embraces the diversity of its congregants. The Muslim community is not a monolithic block. In fact, according to the Pew Research Center, Muslims are the most diverse religious group in America. Of Muslim Americans, 35 percent are born in the United States. The rest hail from Pakistan, Bangladesh, India, Afghanistan, Malaysia, Singapore, Iran, Algeria, Egypt, Syria, Jordan, Morocco, Palestine, Saudi Arabia, the United Arab Emirates, Sudan, Tunisia, Somalia, Yemen, Ghana, Ivory Coast, Senegal, Guinea, Sierra Leone, and, of course, Albania and Turkey—and this is by no means an exhaustive list.[14]

This diversity is addressed in the Qur'an:

> O mankind! We created you from a single (pair) of a male and a female, and made you into nations and tribes, that you may know each other (not that you may despise each

other). Surely the most honoured of you in the sight of
Allah is (he who is) the most righteous of you. And Allah
has full knowledge and is well acquainted (with all things).
(Qur'an 49:13)

Muslims in America are also diverse in socioeconomic
status, education level, and age, and American mosques are
reflective of this diversity. It is the job of the mosque leadership to do their best to provide for all congregants, not just
cater to a few.

A Green Mosque is one in which the elders involve the
young people in making decisions. This helps the community
to stay vibrant, fresh, and poised to grow. The Ash-Shaheed
Islamic Center in Charlotte, North Carolina, exemplifies this
agreement between elders and youth. Green Deen activist
Aidah Muhammad recently spent three years at Ash-Shaheed
and describes it as 'the most progressive community I have
seen, with an emphasis on going green.' The community is also
diverse ethnically, with large numbers of African Americans,
Bengalis, Somalis, Ethiopians, and Arabs.[15]

One of the first decisions the youth at Ash-Shaheed made
was to go green, and the mosque elders gave them the space
and the mentorship to push their ideas. The result was all
stainless steel and energy-efficient appliances and a water-
filtering system that allows the community to bottle water
for themselves. My good friend and environmental scientist/
activist Mohamad Chakaki frequently talks about the challenge of moving forward as a community without good mentorship. At the Ash-Shaheed Islamic Center, however, mentorship of the youth and acceptance of their ability to lead
have developed into the beginnings of a Green Mosque.

A Green Mosque is also one in which the people who use it create zero greenhouse gases in travelling to it. In New York City, where the citizens are predominantly pedestrians, there are almost three hundred mosques.[16] These mosques aren't necessarily green, but the process of getting to them is. For instance, many New York City mosques have had to go cheap on building basics such as carpeting, and thus their rugs are full of volatile organic compounds that add to greenhouse gases. Also, most New York City mosques are converted buildings and thus could benefit from an energy audit and better insulation. However, these mosques rarely have a parking lot, so people get to them by public transport or, better yet, by cycling or walking.

I walk to work, to the gym, and to the mosque. I walk around the crowded streets listening to the calls of the street meat vendors. I walk to buy my groceries and get my wife flowers, and on the way I pass by four or five mosques. So I pray in many places, and I get to all of them on foot. I often pray in a small West African mosque. I also pray at Masjid At-Taqwa, the mosque where I grew up in Brooklyn, a five-minute walk from the West African mosque. Masjid At-Taqwa was founded by a group of twenty-five strong, dedicated African American converts to Islam; my father was one of them. Having a Green Mosque in New York City means being able to walk to it, rather than being stuck in a traffic jam or finding yourself without a space in the parking lot.

Walking to the mosque offers an opportunity to serve God and praise the planet, and part of greening a mosque is to make it easier for people to travel to it without a car. For example, your mosque community might work with local transport officials to site a bus stop near the mosque or to have bike paths and pavements that intersect the mosque so congregants can have choices about the ways they travel to and from it.

No More Styrofoam!
Embracing the Barn-Raising Ethos

Mosques are not only places of worship. They're also places of gathering and therefore places of plentiful eating. Mosques provide ample food for anyone, Muslim or not, especially during Ramadan, the holiest month of the Islamic calendar. It's the month believed to be when the Qur'an was first revealed to the Prophet Muhammad (peace be upon him). In Ramadan, Muslims fast from sunrise to sunset for thirty days. At sunset, communities come together to break the fast with a meal known as the Iftar.

Think of the mosques that host hundreds of people every night in Ramadan for Iftar—using paper towels, paper plates, plastic forks, water from plastic bottles, soda from cans, and tea served in Styrofoam cups. Imagine these mosques instead having reusable dishes and utensils and an industrial dishwasher, with the community pitching in together to clean up after the meal. Doesn't that sound like a greener centre of religious and community life?

In Oakland, California, a small group of committed Muslims pulled together to stop the use of paper plates and the overuse of plastic bottles during Ramadan. Their mosque, the Lighthouse Mosque, was established in 2008 in an old storefront in West Oakland, a low-income neighbourhood that suffers from malnutrition and chronic disease, poverty, and underdevelopment, with limited opportunities for youth.[17]

The Lighthouse community is known for being progressive and environmentally conscious. Their imam, Zaid Shakir,[18] is a world-renowned Muslim American scholar and an 'earthy' family man who rides his bike almost more than he drives. The mosque instituted a 'green Iftar' policy in Ramadan of 2009, beginning with replacing disposable plates with stainless steel ones. Next they began scraping organic waste off the plates into a compost bin. Then teams in the kitchen started separating the trash. Finally, Iftar attendees began bringing their own drinking receptacles, ending the use of bottled water and Styrofoam cups. The whole process is reminiscent of the early American practice of 'barn raising'—in which a whole community would come together to help build each other's barns and other structures. The Lighthouse community's Green Mosque sets an example for all of us. They are following the Green Deen principles of being just toward the Earth (adl) and maintaining balance (mizan) by spreading responsibility across all community members.

Maintaining a Green Mosque requires constant effort. Imagine your local mosque. How much plastic do you think is wasted during Ramadan? How much trash is generated after each meal? Maybe some of these fundamental data points need to be gathered as an initial step to make sure that your mosque community has a quantitative baseline to start from. Then when you take the steps that the Lighthouse Mosque has taken, you can use them to measure your mosque's progress. Eventually, when mosques across the world begin implementing the simple steps taken by the Lighthouse Mosque, green practices will become part of the greater Islamic community everywhere.

Setting Goals to Green Your Mosque

To green a mosque or to maintain a Green Mosque, setting goals is essential. These goals can be numerical. For example, the ADAMS (All Dulles Area Muslim Society) Center Mosque outside of Washington, DC, has published an impressive guide for the propagation of a Green Muslim identity.[19] The guide was released after Ramadan in 2009 and has set an ambitious and important goal: to reduce the ADAMS Center energy and water consumption by 10 percent in 2010 and to cut it by 25 percent by 2013. Let's challenge Muslim communities and mosques across the country to take on similar goals.

Our goals can also be rooted in our personal experience. Some of us recall the blackouts that affected the Northeast in 2003 and left millions without power for days. Let's set a goal to get all mosques 'off the grid' so that even if there is a blackout, in the darkness all mosques will be brilliantly aglow with light. We will explain how to do this in more detail when we look at energy in part II of this book.

Another goal is to live as close as possible to a mosque, perhaps close enough to walk there. There are a number of hadith (sayings of the Holy Prophet) that relate—for example: 'With every step made toward Allah, He runs toward you.'[20] Why not walk to the mosque, help save the Earth, and get closer to Allah in the process?

Another simple goal is one of association. You know that alcohol is *haram* (impermissible). You also know that pork is *haram*. Well, a Green Mosque should also see Polystyrene, plastic bottles, and other throwaway kitchen goods as similarly forbidden. I am not saying they are *haram*. What I am saying is that we can set goals to transform how we serve food in our mosques and find better ways to make sure that hundreds of people eat, all while creating less waste.

By ensuring that our mosques are in balance with their geographic climates, by learning lessons from our diversity of thought, by taking cues from existing Green Mosques, and by setting goals, we can begin to transform mosques around the globe into beacons of eco-friendly and sustainable practices.

You pray there, you eat there, you sleep there. Your children take classes there, and you or your family members even get married there. It's your mosque. Now maybe it's time you transformed the mosque. How green is your mosque?

Part II Watts

Among His Signs is this, that He sends the Winds, as heralds of Glad Tidings, giving you a taste of His (Grace and) Mercy. (Qur'an 30:46)

The blackout of 2003 in the northeastern United States really got me thinking about energy and about the imbalances in the way we deliver energy. I recall the blackout as if it were yesterday. I was at work in Brooklyn's Prospect Park when it happened. I immediately thought of my mother and sister and tried to call them. They both worked at the same hospital across town, and there was no way to reach either of them. I rode my bike to try and catch up with my mother. Eventually, I learned that both she and my sister were safe, but only after much worry and stress. Questions nagged at me and millions of others: Why were the lights out? How did things get so completely out of balance?

Our commitment to living a Green Deen starts with prayer, which is the anchor we have to understanding the Oneness of God and His creation (*tawhid*); seeing and reading His signs (*ayat*); being stewards of the Earth (*khalifah*); honouring the trust we have with God to protect the planet and leave it better than we found it (*amanah*); moving toward justice (*adl*); and maintaining that justice by living in balance and harmony with nature (*mizan*). Our way of life requires balanced management of energy. If we follow the signs of Allah, we can, as stewards of the Earth, find the energy we need in a way that balances earthly resources with our daily human needs.

We derive the power we use from both renewable and nonrenewable sources. The nonrenewable sources I describe as 'energy from hell'. These sources include oil, gas, coal, and nuclear energy—sources we extract from the ground. In contrast, 'energy from heaven' is renewable; it comes from the wind and the sun and from more sustainable consumption practises, including increased efficiency. The call for a green economy and green jobs is about energy from heaven, efficiency, creativity, and innovation.

In these next chapters, by observing the ways in which we provide and consume energy, we can see signs that illuminate the true nature of our relationship with the Earth. There are things we can do to improve this relationship. By focusing on energy from heaven and turning away from energy from hell, by improving the efficiency of what we already do, by innovating in the green economy, and by imagining and practising living off the grid, we can truly be in concert with nature and do justice to the land, the air, and the sea—and to ourselves.

In these chapters I will also touch on the 2010 massive BP oil well spill in the Gulf of Mexico. I hope to offer a reasonable way forward, whose roots may be found in the combined efforts of all sectors of our society to do whatever it takes to ensure that a disaster of this magnitude never happens again.

What are some of the ways that we can *use* the light of Allah—which He gave us in the form of the Qur'an and the sunnah of the Prophet (peace be upon him)—combined with the light of electricity that He willed us to find as His stewards on Earth?

Chapter 5

Energy from Hell

Energy from hell is energy that is derived from the ground. It is extracted from the Earth, it is dirty, and it is a major cause of pollution and climate change. Energy from hell is nonrenewable; it takes away from the Earth without giving back. It disturbs the balance (*mizan*) of the universe and is therefore a great injustice (*zulm*). A Green Deen calls for maintaining the Earth's balance and treating it justly.

In Islam, Allah calls all people to justice (*adl*):

> O you who believe! Stand out firmly for justice, as witnesses to Allah, even as against yourselves, or your parents, or your kin, and whether it be (against) rich or poor: for Allah can best protect both. Follow not the lusts (of your hearts), lest you swerve, and if you distort (justice) or decline to do justice, verily Allah is well-acquainted with all that you do. (Qur'an 4:135)

One way we can stand out firmly for justice is by ending our reliance on oil and coal. Energies from hell are particularly devastating and unjust to people and the planet. Oil and coal are toxic to water, sky, and ground. In this chapter, I focus on oil and coal as examples of energies from hell that those aiming for a Green Deen should avoid.

Oil

Oil is ubiquitous. Oil companies are some of the most profitable organisations in the world. Most people on the planet use oil in some way. There is almost no one on the planet who does not consume oil in transportation, in heating their home, or in goods that are processed with oil, such as plastics. Since we are all involved in creating the demand for oil, each of us can also be involved in a decision to limit the use of oil. This decision has taken on added significance since the devastating effects of the 2010 BP oil spill in the Gulf of Mexico.

Oil and International Conflict: Iran

The places where oil is most prevalent also happen to be where international conflicts occur—for example, Iraq, Iran, and Nigeria. Let's consider the case of Iran. The obsession with controlling the Persian nation's oil reserves has led to a tumultuous, unstable, and threatening political relationship between Iran and the West.

Oil was first discovered in Iran in 1908 and was controlled by the Anglo-Persian Oil Company, which today is known as BP. Over time, the Iranian people became resentful, for they never saw the profits of their land's natural resource, and when a new generation of post–World War II Iranians came to power, they decided the time had come to manage their own natural resources.

In 1951, Mohammad Mossadegh became the popularly

elected prime minister of Iran and oversaw the nationalisation of oil production, following which the company name was changed to the Anglo-Iranian Oil Company—one of its many name changes. This bold step on behalf of Mossadegh angered international oil interests, who had used Iranian oil to power two world wars.

An international boycott followed, along with political turmoil inside Iran. In 1953, the U.S. Central Intelligence Agency succeeded in overthrowing the popularly elected government of Iran, which had nationalised the oil industry."[1] This coup caused further internal political instability, political upheaval, and, ultimately, the Iranian Revolution, which overthrew the U.S.-backed Pahlavi monarchy and installed an Islamist government.

That Islamic Republic of Iran currently controls its oil and continues to have a hostile relationship with the United States.[2] Countries all over the world have suffered similar wars, international corporate involvements, repressive governments, and political instability—all thanks to the extraction of oil and its overconsumption.

Domestic Oil and the Balance of Nature: Alaska and the Gulf of Mexico

Current domestic examples of the disturbance of the balance in nature and the resulting injustice linked to oil extraction can be seen in the Alaska National Wildlife Refuge and in the Gulf of Mexico, where our dependency on oil is threatening and destroying the natural balance of life (*mizan*).

In Alaska, the air is clean, the water is clean, and the land is virtually untouched. Underneath this immaculate earth exist

plentiful oil, coal, and natural gas. The Alaska National Wildlife Refuge is home to the Gwich'in people, whose ancestors
have lived in the region for generations.[3] I recently spoke with
Faith Gemmill, who grew up in a small village about two hundred miles north of Fairbanks, Alaska.[4] Called the Arctic Village, Faith's hometown is the northernmost Native American
community in America. It is one of the smallest villages in all
of Alaska and is surrounded by mountains on all sides. When
Faith was growing up, her life (and survival) revolved around
the seasons: springtime fishing, summer and fall gathering of
berries, and caribou hunting in the fall.

Our dependency on oil threatens human life. For example,
Faith noted that rates of asthma, hyperthyroidism, and breast
cancer in Alaska have multiplied exponentially as the quest
to extract Alaska's oil has grown. While there is no proven
direct causation, there is certainly a correlation between the
appearance of the oil industry, the stress it has caused, and the
health of the local people.

Local Alaskans are fighting some of the largest oil companies in the world. In 1988, Faith's Native American nation
organised themselves to protect their homeland. Elders called
a meeting, gathering chiefs from every village. Faith recalls
that 'no one was really talking about global warming. Our people knew already that it was coming; our leaders were talking
about it back then [in 1988].' As an adult, Faith helped develop
a network called Resisting Environmental Destruction on
Indigenous Land, or REDOIL.

At the turn of the twenty-first century, a new player arrived
on the Alaskan oil scene—Shell Oil. Shell wants to begin drilling offshore in Alaska. The struggle for balance between the

Alaska National Wildlife Refuge and justice for Alaska's people continues. If you want to support the communities in Alaska that are working to maintain the delicate balance of nature, then support Resisting Environmental Destruction on Indigenous Lands (REDOIL).

Let me be very clear and speak plainly about the 2010 BP oil spill in the Gulf of Mexico, because this is where the issue of our societal dependence on oil and our personal choices converge. First, let us keep in mind the central principle of our Green Deen, *tawhid*—that there is one God, one humanity, and one humanity serving the One God. Our reaction and response to the BP oil spill must be within this understanding. The spill came as a devastating reminder that the price of our fossil fuel dependence is far too high. We must not let history repeat itself. Although the path is muddled, and fraught with many unintended consequences that we must be prepared for, I feel that the trust (*amanah*) we have with God to be protectors of the planet demands that we declare our independence from energy from hell and reduce the environmental harm we are seeing in the Gulf of Mexico.

The BP oil spill, a seafloor gusher resulting from the 20 April 2010 explosion of a deepwater drilling rig, billowed thousands of barrels of crude oil into the ocean each day for almost three months causing widespread damage to marine and wildlife habitats along the Gulf Coast and to the area's fishing and tourism industries. Although as this book went to press in early August 2010, the wellhead had been sealed, National Oceanic and Atmospheric Administration (NOAA) estimates that 4.9 million barrels of oil had spilled into the Gulf,[5] and the effects on the ecology in the Gulf and its fisheries, the impacts on the economic system, and the health consequences of this spill will not truly be known for many years.[6]

The photographs of how the oil has affected the Gulf coast and the birds and fish that live there inspire one to think of who is ultimately accountable. Determining accountability is murky, and both BP and the U.S. federal government have taken a share of the blame. People must also look to U.S. offshore drilling policy, the actions of governments around the world, and the ever-rising global demand for oil. We all have some culpability, and we must all be involved in the resulting solutions.

Coal

Coal is the main source of the electricity that powers our lives. Think about how many televisions are in your home right now. Perhaps there is one in the living room, one in each bedroom, and maybe another smaller one in the kitchen. Now think about computers and laptops. How many does your household have? What about mobile phones? All these devices need to be plugged in and charged up, right? If you live in a region where electricity comes from a coal-fired plant, each time something surges with power, the source is coal.

Living a Green Deen requires us to know the science behind the many processes that power our lives. The process of burning coal to create electricity begins in a power plant, where coal is ground up into a fine powder. When this powder is burned, it generates steam, which provides power to a turbine engine that powers a generator. The generator uses magnets and metals like copper and aluminium to create a flow of electrons—tiny atomic particles. This is electricity.[7]

Electricity is measured in watts. The more electricity you use, the more watts you consume. A 60-watt light bulb uses more electricity than a 45-watt light bulb. The 60-watt bulb is brighter and creates more light than the 45-watt bulb. Therefore, the 60-watt bulb also requires more coal to create a larger flow of electrons to produce the electricity that creates the light. Think of big cities like New York, Los Angeles, and Chicago. Think of the amount of electricity they use. Forget watts; city use of electricity is measured in megawatts (millions of watts) or gigawatts—billions of watts![8] Since coal is cheap and readily available, it's used to power, these huge cities.

Coal is an impressive source of power but it comes at a catastrophic cost.

Allah says:

And it is He who spread out the earth, and set thereon mountains standing firm, and flowing rivers. (Qur'an 13:3)

As His representatives, we must protect the Earth, including its mountains and what's inside the mountains.

Mountaintop Removal Coal Mining

Traditionally, when we think of coal mining, we think of men tunneling deep into the core of a mountain and extracting the black rock from below. That process has always been fraught with danger. Today, in the Appalachian region of the United States, the majority of coal mining is done by mountaintop removal, a practice that has grown exponentially in the last fifteen years. Coal companies such as the Massey Corporation literally blow the tops off mountains to gain quick access to coal. Mountaintop removal mining saves money for coal companies because less human labour is needed to extract coal from the inside of a mountain (once its top is blown off) than to drill below a mountain, but it creates open sores on the Earth. According to iLoveMountains.org:

> Mountaintop removal mining, if it continues unabated, will cause a projected loss of 1.4 million acres of land by the end of the decade—an area the size of Delaware—with a concomitant severe impact on fish, wildlife, and bird species, not to mention a devastating effect on many neighboring communities.[9]

Mountaintop removal coal mining is an extremely destructive practice, harmful both to the environment and to humanity.

When the top of a mountain is blown off, the rubble goes deep into valleys, covering streams and communities that live in those valleys. The rubble consists of boulders, known as 'flyrock', and ash. At all steps and stages of mining for coal, there are concerns about huge boulders that can kill people. In fact, Jeremy Davidson, a three-year-old child, was one such casualty. In 2004, Jeremy was sleeping in his bed in his home in Inman, Virginia, when A&G Coal was widening a road at a mine site and a dislodged boulder rolled down the mountainside and into the Davidson home, killing young Jeremy. The family received $3 million in settlements and left the region.[10]

In the small town of Sylvester, West Virginia, the coal company had to install a huge nylon dome over the coal processing plant because it was creating so much coal dust in the town that a parked car, after only an hour, would be covered in three inches of coal dust.[11] This dust is known to cause 'black lung', a term applied to a number of respiratory diseases that can lead to severe illness or death.

In addition to rubble and ash, mountaintop removal mining results in flooding. When it rains, water is supposed to be absorbed by the soil and tree roots and other vegetation that grows on mountaintops and mountainsides. When a mountaintop is removed, rain goes straight down into the valleys below, increasing the volume of the streams by three to five times, resulting in flooding.[12] Imagine being flooded out of your home multiple times a year. Many people turn off their televisions when it starts raining so they can hear the speed of the water and therefore gauge how serious it sounds—will it flood or not? Not knowing the answer, many have decided to sleep in their clothes so they can leave quickly in case of a flood.

Mountaintop removal mining also contributes to the depletion of water sources. Coal companies have already buried close to two thousand miles of Appalachian streams beneath piles of toxic waste and debris.[13] According to Mary Anne Hitt, deputy director of the Sierra Club's Beyond Coal Campaign, swift and decisive action is necessary to protect communities' waterways from mountaintop removal. 'The slow timetable to protect waterways from mining waste will mean more destruction in Appalachia', she predicts.[14]

Mountaintop removal mining has had a devastating effect on towns like Inman and Sylvester in West Virginia, which are far from the public consciousness. They are small, buried in mountain ranges, and extremely poor. Coal companies either buy out an entire community (it then simply ceases to exist) or just set up shop and start mining. Some companies slowly buy up the mountains around the town and circle in like an encroaching army. Locals can try (and have tried) to fight coal companies from starting operations in their hometown, but their efforts are usually unsuccessful. Seemingly nothing can impede the process of coal companies' capturing as much coal as they possibly can to maximise their profits, except perhaps our reduced use of electricity. Coal operations can deplete thousands and thousands of acres and reach across multiple miles.[15]

The use of energies from hell contradicts every principle of a Green Deen. A Green Deen sees the Earth as a mosque. A Green Deen commands us to move toward justice (*adl*), to respect the balance of nature (*mizan*), and to be stewards of the planet (*khalifah*). Extracting oil and coal from the Earth destroys the delicate balance of the natural world. The toxicity created from oil drilling and mountaintop removal mining destroys people's lives unjustly. Using the world for its resources in this way is not good stewardship.

A Green Deen chooses connection over disconnection from the Earth. When we harm the natural world around us, we destroy the connection we have to the planet. When we clear forests for coal mining, we risk destroying the signs (*ayat*) of God in nature. Even though coal company executives say that they are reforesting, in reality they're dismantling a house and only rebuilding the frame. You cannot repair the damage you are doing; you must stop creating the damage in the first place. A Green Deen avoids the use of energies from hell and supports the use of energies from heaven.

What You Can Do

One thing you can do to avoid using energies from hell is to conduct an energy audit of your energy use. If you are involved in the leadership of your local mosque or Muslim community centre, then do the same. Lower your energy use. Turn off those lights. Get more involved in the fight against using coal, especially against mountaintop removal coal mining. Support the Ohio Valley Environmental Coalition, the Coal River Wind Project, or the continued efforts of the Sierra Club.

The answers lie in this shared sense of responsibility. Because we are all connected in the Oneness of creation and are all stewards of the planet, seeing the signs of Allah in nature so cruelly devastated can move us toward an expression of the best of the environmental movement. To solve these problems, the combined effort of all sectors of society is required.

It requires the public sector (governments at all levels) to create policies that spur innovation away from fossil fuels. It requires the private sector (corporations big and small) to transform their business models so that the potential negative impacts to the environment are factored into their growth and development. It requires the civic sector (nonprofits and nongovernmental and religious organisations) to aid in the cleanup, and to participate in the public education that will transform the way citizens understand their own personal actions.

Finally, it will take you, the individual. Keep in mind the Alaska National Wildlife Refuge, the Gulf of Mexico oil spill, West Virginia, and other areas ravaged by industry to produce goods we all consume. Keep the people now out of work in your prayers. Drive less and use products that are not petroleum based.

A Green Deen stands in support of the people who are protecting their land from invasive companies that value profits over people. These companies create havoc and unbalance the planet, and it is up to you to be the solution. There are countless West Virginias and Alaskas and Gulf of Mexicos around the world where nature is being carved up to extract oil and coal and other raw materials. Just looking at the Gulf of Mexico oil spill should remind us that there are currently almost four thousand offshore drilling platforms operational in the Gulf.[16] Using less energy transforms the demand for oil and coal. If everyone collectively used less energy, we might begin to move from energy from hell toward energy from heaven.

What can you do to declare your independence from energy from hell?

Chapter 6

Energy from Heaven

Energy from heaven comes from above. It is not extracted from the Earth, and it is renewable. On 27 September 2008, over fifty thousand Americans in seven hundred communities across the fifty United States stood up and said, 'America is ready to build the new economy. We're ready to save people and the planet. We're ready for green jobs now!' One of those seven hundred communities was the Anacostia community outside of Washington, DC. At the Anacostia Green Jobs Now rally, Mike Tidwell, director of the Chesapeake Climate Action Network, noticed he was speaking on the lawn of a church and said, 'We need to get our energy from heaven, wind, solar, and waves, instead of from hell—the stuff in the ground like coal, oil, and gas.'[1]

Extraction causes imbalance, whereas energy from above is like a gift from heaven. In this chapter, we discuss how a Green Deen affirms that Islam is a path that opens your heart to the Oneness of God and His creation (*tawhid*), a path that calls humans to see the signs of God (*ayat*), to be stewards of the earth (*khalifah*), and to honour the trust we have with God to be protectors of the planet (*amanah*). A Green Deen acknowledges that God created everything in perfect balance (*mizan*), that humans are made to perfectly coexist on the Earth, and that disturbing this balance is the fundamental form of injustice (*zulm*). Our Green Deen is Islam, the religion of 1.4 billion people around the world, and it requires bringing the world into a state of balance in respect to how we consume and manage energy.

Gifts from the Sun

Solar power is one example of energy from heaven. Solar power is as old as the Earth itself. It is plentiful, free, and possibly inexhaustible. To the faithful, the only power that could blot out the sun is the power that made it. Muslims do not look to the sun with reverence; instead, we look to it with awe as one of the signs of Allah's power, might, and mercy. There is even a surah (chapter) in the Qur'an named after the sun—the Surah al-Shams, or Chapter of the Sun. It speaks in part to the sun's overwhelming importance and power.

My interest in Surah al-Shams was strengthened as I did research for this book. I have often heard it recited during prayer times at the various mosques that I walk to in New York City, and one week I heard this surah recited in three out of the five daily prayers. That same week, I wandered into a small mosque in Brooklyn, gave salaams (greetings) to the old men who are often there to pray, and walked over to the stack of Qur'ans. I wanted to learn Surah al-Shams.

Muslims believe that the power of the Qur'an gives understanding of the power of everything in God's creation. In thinking about how our imams guide us when we're learning to read Qur'an, it occurred to me that we should similarly be seeking experts in alternative and renewable energy—engineers and product designers—to guide us in seeking how to gather energy from heaven.

My process of learning Surah al-Shams required my seeking help from a local imam. Also named Ibrahim, the imam I consulted is a Hafiz, one who has memorised the entire Qur'an. His recitation is clear and startling and makes your hair stand on end. He recited, and I repeated. If I faltered, he would read the line again, and I would repeat it again and again until I got it right.

Remember that *ayah*s are both signs of God and verses of the Qur'an. Both are meant for reflection. It was when I was in a deep state of reflection regarding this book that Surah al-Shams began to appear repeatedly in my life.

In the name of Allah, the Most Beneficent, the Most Merciful

By the Sun and his (glorious) splendour
By the Moon as she follows him
By the Day as it shows up (the Sun's) glory;
By the Night as it conceals it;
By the firmament and its (wonderful) structure;
By the Earth and its (wide) expanse:
By the Soul, and the proportion and order given to it;
And its enlightenment as to its wrong and its right—
Truly he succeeds that purifies it,
And he Fails that corrupts it!
(Qur'an 91:1–15)

The sun has been our natural partner for growth and inspiration. It provides both light and heat and serves as a reminder that God is more powerful than anything human beings can create. Qur'an translator and commentator Abdullah Yusuf

Ali calls those first ten lines of Surah al-Shams 'a fine nature passage.'[2] For me, this fine nature passage has been a glorious source of inspiration. If God can mention 'the Sun and his (glorious) splendour', what can we as humans do today to absorb some of that splendour? How can we use the sun to energise our lives?

In modern times, we can harness the power of the sun through two systems of solar energy. Passive, or thermal, systems store, collect, and move heat. Photovoltaic systems convert sunlight into electricity.[3] Either of these systems can fit on your roof. So if you own your own home or building, you can easily find a solar company to install one of them. The process takes just a few days. Larger models also exist, such as Florida's DeSoto Next Generation Solar Energy Center. With ninety thousand solar panels, it is the largest solar power plant in the United States.

Yusef Miller and Barbara Grant are Green Muslims and experts in distributed generation—the on-site generation of electricity from many small energy sources. The motto of their company, Photovoltaic Products Plus (PPS), is 'Changing the World One Solar Panel at a Time.'[4] Yusef and Barbara began by installing solar panels on homes here in the United States, but for the past two years they have turned their attention to the West African nation of Sierra Leone. Today, PPS is negotiating with the Sierra Leonean government to install solar street lights throughout the capital.[5] Sierra Leone wants to grow and improve technologically, but affordably. Solar power addresses a critical energy need while remaining affordable and safe for the environment.

You can do two things to follow the Sierra Leone model. First, encourage your local and state officials to upgrade electricity systems so excess energy is pushed back into the grid, and lobby them to clear political hurdles standing in the way of localised solar power adoption. Second, get involved in the industry.

Getting involved in the solar industry can mean many different things on both the supply and demand sides. Let's start with research and development. If you are blessed to have resources yourself, or are in a position to leverage dollars from an academic institution or agency, you can support the research and development of new technologies to improve the delivery of solar power. Another way you can get involved is to start a company that supports the solar industry. Think holistically about this—each industry needs raw materials, public relations, and marketing, and it needs installers. There are ample opportunities to help build the solar industry and be a active part of its growth.

Solar energy is in need of the brightest minds to make the technology affordable so it can be expanded to the scale required to power millions more lives than it does today. Some of the brightest minds are those who score high in science, maths, and engineering; who understand how systems work; and who are problem solvers and project managers. Are you one of these people? Perhaps you thought that your only viable path was to go into medicine, law, or traditional engineering. We need the brightest minds to approach the biggest challenge that we have faced in our time—energy management. Using the power of the sun, which God has made plentiful for us, is a great challenge that must be met by the smartest amongst us. Are you one of these bright minds?

Investment in solar technology is a smart move for those (bright minds included) looking to green their Deen, their path toward connecting with the One Creator of everything in the entire universe. The Deen of Islam affirms the Oneness of all in creation (*tawhid*) and compels us to maintain the delicate balance (*mizan*) that God created so that we can maintain justice (*adl*) in all that we do. Solar power helps us to maintain this balance because it is an already existing resource that could have no negative impact on the planet.

As it is now, we still need to extract materials from the ground to produce the electricity. Investment in solar technology will begin to unlock the potential of the sun as a viable resource. Investment can come in the form of a financial investment (stock in already existing companies or by seeding a good idea) or by investing time in helping build demand— either by installing panels at your home or place of work or worship or by investing in the political process and working for policies that can unhinge local laws to make solar power more viable.

Not only is solar power an energy from heaven, it comes in multiple forms, and it can be used at a single location or to cover a wide area. It is a developing technology that has become more profitable in recent years. Living a Green Deen does not necessarily mean living off the electrical grid. It can mean living smartly on the grid. Investing in solar power is one such way to be smart, and the investment process can bring in people who are not traditionally thought of as parties interested in a healthier planet.

Wind We Can Use

Wind power is another example of energy from heaven. Allah says in the Qur'an:

Among His Signs is this, that He sends the Winds, as heralds of Glad Tidings, giving you a taste of His (Grace and) Mercy. (Qur'an 30:46)

Wind is like a gift, or good news, from God. Scholars have also interpreted this verse to mean that wind is the messenger of rain, and rain is the blessing that gives us our crops. The same verse continues:

that the ships may sail (majestically) by His Command and that you may seek of His Bounty: in order that you may be grateful. (Qur'an 30:46)

Here God is noting that the wind is powerful enough to push ships through the ocean and that this force is a part of His bounty for humanity. Islam seems tailor-made to capture the power of the wind.

Some Native American reservations have successfully harnessed wind power and can serve as examples for the rest of us. Winona LaDuke, the Green Party's vice presidential nominee in the 1996 and 2000 presidential elections, is a Native American activist and environmentalist who is dedicated to bringing environmentalism and spirituality together. She is not a Muslim but a person who sees the value of bringing faith-based communities into the environmental movement, and she is a human being who embodies the spirit of the Green Deen principle of being a steward of the Earth—particularly of the land she now lives on, which her ancestors also lived on.

As a woman who is native to North America, Winona has spent a lifetime working to connect people to the core (universal) spiritual principles of Oneness (*tawhid*), stewardship (*khalifah*), and the covenant humans have with God to protect the planet (*amanah*). Noting that we have slipped away from that understanding, she remarked at a Green Party presidential campaign appearance in 2000, 'We need to renegotiate our relationship with the Earth.'[6] LaDuke's White Earth Land Recovery Project uses wind turbines to provide power on the White Earth Indians' ancestral lands.[7] Neighbours from surrounding areas began to take notice and eventually solicited the tribe's help in providing wind power for their own farms as well.

I met Winona LaDuke in 2008 at the Good Jobs, Green Jobs conference in Washington, DC. Over a meal she told me, 'It turns out that reservations around the USA are on some of the windiest land in the country.'[8] The wind power available on Indian lands was also noted more recently in an article in a leading and arguably impartial magazine, the *Economist*, which in 2010 reported that 'tribes in Montana and North Dakota have enough wind to generate more than 886 megawatt hours a year.'[9]

Ten years ago, in 2000, LaDuke called for a renegotiation of our relationship with the Earth. Today, in 2010, Native American reservations are doing just that and are serving as examples that even the *Economist* can get behind.

The 'Smart Grid'

A central question in switching to energy from heaven is whether the electricity grid can manage the surge of new power coming from non-traditional sources. The grid is antiquated. It can barely manage our current unbalanced use of electricity. Could it manage our transformation to energy delivery that is more balanced?

One morning I woke up to drilling outside my house. I learned that the electricity was off in my apartment and that the men outside were drilling to find the problem. The eighty-year-old wires that I depend on for lights are part of an interconnected electrical grid, and when something goes wrong, it's hard to find the source of the problem. The foresight to create an interconnected electrical grid in the last century was impressive. But now, almost a hundred years later, we are left with an ageing system that has been underfunded and deprioritised. In its current state, our electrical grid is unable to manage energies from heaven. But there is a solution, if we are dedicated to changing our ways.

A system that can manage new sources of energy is called a 'smart grid'. It's smart because it can monitor and track how people use and produce energy.[10] The smart grid can be a tool for balancing the old and the new and for determining the best source of energy in a particular situation. As I was researching the smart grid for this chapter, I came across hundreds of writings by Massoud Amin. Amin, an Iranian American engineer, is an expert on the American electrical grid. He is also credited for coining the term 'smart grid', a phrase that has now become ubiquitous. It was popular on the 2008 campaign trail and is still a central feature of IBM advertisements. The popular ads have the tagline 'Building a Smarter Planet' and show how data can be culled from almost any source—a street, a building, even a baby in a nursery.

Data over time can lead to extrapolation and predictions and eventually smarter decisions over how to allocate resources. Remember when I made the call for all you bright people out there? Well, this is also where we need you. Whether you are in the United States, China, India, Brazil,

Turkey, France, or Nigeria, making the best use of our renewable energy resources requires us to have a smarter grid that can give us more information. Are you up for this challenge?

In Green Deen terms, a smarter grid means that to use energies from heaven effectively, we need a grid that will be as advanced as the energy is. Even venture capitalist Haider Akmal knows that smart grids are critical. 'Ultimately', Haider stressed, 'the big thing is how to build a smart grid. You can leave those ancient wires in the ground, and you will still need to build [transformers] that will measure peak hours. There needs to be a demand response that gives the utility the power to have a two-way communication to modulate power consumption.'[11]

Yes, it sounds complicated when explained in venture capitalist–speak. But the state of the electrical grid today could be compared to listening to music on a phonograph and an old 33 rpm record. To play today's MP3s, we need an iPod.

Green or Brown?

There are three questions to ask yourself when trying to determine whether an energy source is compatible with a Green Deen:

1. Is it clean at the point of capture and at the point of use?
2. Is it renewable?
3. Will it make people sick?

Some tout nuclear energy as clean energy because it does not produce any carbon emissions. However, that perspective fails to account for the extraction of the fissile material from the ground, the transport of material to the power plant, and the disposal of it after it has been spent in the fission.[12] Wave power is promising, but it is a science that is nearly half a century in the future. We have to be realistic about what choices we can make now. Supporting sourcing that is cleaner is a great step. Investing in the long term in sources that are clean and have minimal impact is better. At the end of the day, energies from heaven—in this case, solar and wind power—are the new approaches to solving the age-old problem of how to provide light, heat, and other luxuries we enjoy.

Each of us has a role in supporting clean energy through the products we buy. Are they energy-efficient? Simple steps like turning down the thermostat, switching appliances off, walking or taking public transport, even air-drying your clothes instead of using the dryer can all reduce energy consumption. Also important is your consciousness that electricity is not always a renewable resource—it should not be taken for granted.

As we begin to renegotiate our relationship with the planet and align ourselves with Green Deen principles such as living in balance with nature (*mizan*) and the Oneness of God and His creation (*tawhid*), we should seek energies that come seemingly straight from God. The management of energy has always been a challenge. Humans have used their own power to build pyramids and the power of fossil fuels to go to the moon. We have learned by doing. If today we harness the power of the sun and the wind, perhaps we will protect ourselves, one another, and the planet so that we can praise God for many more days.

What are the ways that you are already prepared to be actively engaged in the green energy movement? How can you promote, support, or develop clean energy from heaven? Let's think about solutions—how can you be part of the solution and where can you limit or reduce your reliance on energy from hell?

The fate of our energy future depends on you! Will it be energy from heaven or energy from hell? Choose wisely.

Chapter 7

Efficiency and Green Jobs

Green jobs and a green economy have the potential to transform our society from an economic system that is reliant on pollution to one that is cleaner and greener and that fulfills our responsibility as stewards of the Earth (*khalifah*). In 2007, the term 'green jobs' was barely seen or heard, but the concept took the nation by storm in the 2008 presidential election. National advocacy organisations involved in the environmental movement joined forces to advance a national campaign calling for 'Green Jobs Now'. The leading organisations were 1Sky, Al Gore's We Campaign, and Green For All.[1] By the end of 2008, 'green jobs' had become a mainstream phrase. Each presidential candidate needed a position on green jobs, which Americans had come to see as a critical solution to pressing problems like global climate change and the failing economy.

This chapter demystifies the green jobs movement and critiques and gives examples of how green jobs and the green economy are deeply rooted in the Islamic ethical principles that command us to embrace justice (*adl*), to honour our covenant with God as protectors of the planet (*amanah*), and to refrain from corrupting the delicate balance of nature (*mizan*). To those in the environmental movement, the green economy movement does what they have been seeking for a long time—that is, it assigns value by how a good or a service impacts on both the planet and the health of humankind. The green economy is about looking widely at what we are already doing and determining if a process is wasteful and harmful—to people and to the planet, the principle of the Oneness of all creation (*tawhid*).

Islam and the green economy are compatible because Islam teaches us that each individual has value simply because each person's soul comes from Allah.

In the Qur'an, Allah says:

There is no soul but has a protector over it. (Qur'an 86:4)

That protector is God.

Activist Joel Rogers, director of the Center on Wisconsin Strategy, has also noted that, historically, times of increased economic activity have coincided with moments of increased efficiency.[2] A green economy is also synonymous with an efficient economy: green jobs help us use our resources better.

Resourcefulness and efficiency are the basic elements of a green economy.[3] The Muslim precedent for resourcefulness comes directly from the hadith of Prophet Muhammad (peace be upon him). During the epic one-day Battle of Uhud, the Holy Prophet (peace be upon him) was injured. His youngest daughter Fatima (peace be upon her) saw that he was bleeding from the mouth. She had her husband, Ali (peace be upon him), bring water to address the wound. But the bleeding did not stop with washing. So Fatima reached for a mat of date palm, burned it, and used the ashes to dress the wound. She was resourceful—she assessed what was available and used it the best way she knew how.[4]

Efficiency, on the other hand, is about saving resources and saving money. Energy efficiency decreases the energy inputs—electricity, heat, or fuel—needed to produce lighting, heating, and cooling. Greater efficiency is achieved when energy waste is reduced and when energy-using systems operate at maximum efficiency.[5]

In effect, resourcefulness is using what you have, and efficiency is using what you have carefully. Both are practices that protect the planet. The green economy is a win-win in a Green Deen—the path that affirms the natural connection between protecting the planet and praising God.

The creation of green jobs is the third layer in a multilayered environmental movement that holds public, private, and civic sectors accountable for increasing efficiency. Recall, the environmental movement first established regulations on waste and watts (energy), then targeted the unsustainable practices of corporations. Each step was a response to our overconsumptive ways and was designed to help us enter into a better relationship with our planet.

For a Green Deen, we need to find examples in which the opportunity of the green economy meets the emphasis on justice in the environmental justice movement. One such example is Green City Force, a Brooklyn-based organisation committed to increasing the number of green jobs and improving the efficiency of buildings. According to the U.S. Green Building Council, the majority of greenhouse gases are emitted from buildings.[6] Green City Force uses experts to train young adults in weatherisation techniques. Trainees are taught to assess whether a home is leaking energy and how to prevent it from leaking more energy—that is, how to make the building more efficient. Weatherisation includes improving insulation, sealing cracks in walls, replacing ageing boilers, and changing old windows. The trainees are young people who have had a tough time finding work and are looking for an opportunity to learn new skills in a burgeoning field. Green City Force works in a variety of neighbourhoods but targets disadvantaged neighbourhoods of Brooklyn.

President Obama has funded the Weatherization Assistance Program specifically to help low-income homeowners improve the energy efficiency of their homes. This approach comes out of efforts by groups like Green For All and puts the government in the position of moving toward justice directly through its green policy. Justice in this case is giving jobs to those that need them and helping those in need to save money by reducing their energy bills.

Community Power and Opportunity— Green Re-entry

Muslims are active participants in the creation of green jobs. A quintessential example of how the Green Deen principles of embracing justice and caring for both planet and people can combine is Chicago's Inner-City Muslim Action Network (IMAN). This organisation started ten years ago in response to the need to prevent black and immigrant (Latino, South Asian, Arab) youths on the south side of Chicago from joining gangs. IMAN's executive director, Rami Nashashibi, a charismatic Palestinian in his thirties, and board member Rafi Peterson, an African American ex-offender in his sixties, joined forces to reach out to these young people. Today

IMAN is one of the most successful social justice organisations to come out of a Muslim community in more than thirty
years.

I spent all of 2009 researching IMAN's model—and
learned that it incorporates service, organising, and the arts.
IMAN has a free health-screening clinic, provides job readi-
ness classes for local residents—mostly non-Muslim—and
conducts monthly artist gatherings to bring the different
parts of the Muslim and non-Muslim communities together.

IMAN's Green Reentry Project aims to help men transitioning out of prison to stay out of prison and successfully
re-enter their communities. IMAN board member Rafi
Peterson started Project Restore, under IMAN's umbrella
of service work. Along with Ma'alam Abdullah, the project's
coordinator, Rafi is training ex-offenders to be at the forefront of the green economy. Project Restore has a distinct
environmental and human justice lens. I stayed at the Project
Restore Transitional House in February 2009. There I was
surrounded by beautiful Muslim brothers who pledged to
do no drinking, smoking, or cursing and to maintain regular prayers and cook and clean for one another. This home is
a safe space for formerly incarcerated Muslim men who are
committed to stabilising themselves and their community as
they return to it.

Five of these Muslim brothers would soon be working with
contractors and architects to learn about energy efficiency in
buildings and to remodel a bungalow purchased by IMAN as
the new transitional home for Project Restore. The original
residents of the first Project Restore house now act as managers of the project to construct the Green Reentry home. They
also help the community by rehabilitating houses that, when

vacant, attracted illegal activity. These men bring light in the form of energy-efficient materials and heating and cooling systems, and they are even planning on drilling and using geothermal energy—energy derived from the heat of the Earth. Once the men have completed the bungalow according to LEED (Leadership in Energy and Environmental Design) green building standards, they plan on getting it LEED certified.

Each man will receive financial support in this process of transitioning post-incarceration. Funding for the project is coming from the city of Chicago through a Community Development Block Grant, which is money connected to the federal stimulus. African American Muslim men coming out of prison are essentially going to be building their own home in the south side of Chicago and making sure that it is done in a way that is good for the planet.

IMAN has plans to expand its green jobs initiative and hopes to continue greening homes and proving ex-offenders jobs to do so. It has purchased two new properties that it plans to turn into a restaurant and an office building, using the green tools and techniques learned from the renovation of the bungalows.

Building the Demand for Green Jobs

The White House is committed to strengthening the demand for green jobs. The current lack of demand resulted in a 2009 White House summit on green jobs, hosted by the White House Council on Environmental Quality and then special White House adviser on green jobs Van Jones. The Departments of Labor, Energy, and Housing and Urban

Development (HUD) and the U.S. Environmental Protection Agency (EPA) all attended the meeting. Van Jones called it 'The effort to repower America and to home-grow our energy.'[7]

Opportunities created from this summit include HUD's receiving a $1 billion grant to green public housing and the Department of Labor's commitment to using dollars for retrofitting buildings—thereby creating job opportunities for many. To support this commitment, the Council on Environmental Quality released a report called *Recovery Through Retrofit*.[8] This report found that more than 130 million homes in the United States generate over 20 percent of the nation's carbon dioxide emissions, making these homes a significant contributor to global climate change. Furthermore, the report found that home energy efficiency retrofits have the potential to reduce home energy bills by $21 billion annually, thus paying for themselves over time.

The White House plans to implement policies to make retrofitting homes attractive to homeowners. Continued policy initiatives aim to drive demand, create jobs, and allow businesses opportunities to innovate. However, if the effort for green jobs is not always linked to justice and equality, it risks perpetuating systems of inequality that it has an opportunity to alleviate.

Muslim or non-Muslim, everyone can be a part of the green jobs movement. However, the net gain that we can get in terms of jobs created will only happen as industry improves its processes, people are retrained, and new people are integrated into the workforce. People of faith can be active in this effort. Mosques and other houses of worship can be retrofitted. Homes can be assessed for energy efficiency.

We need more organisations like IMAN and Green City Force that are able to train people on the fringe of economic prosperity and give them a chance at financial stability. Green jobs help people transition from a pollution-based economy to a sustainable one. Good green jobs maximise community benefits, extend into career ladders, and build pathways out of poverty. Green jobs—creating them and being employed in them—align perfectly with a Green Deen. These jobs help us move toward justice by providing opportunities for the marginalised and by being resourceful and efficient. These jobs help people connect with the natural world.

How green is your job?

Chapter 8

Living Off the Grid

I began this section on watts by talking about the blackout of 2003 in the northeastern United States and how it got me thinking about energy. Throughout this section, we have looked at the sources of present and future energy, and also at energy from heaven versus energy from hell. I have also talked about the promise of green jobs and energy efficiency. Now I want to return to the blackout to talk about how we can address the imbalances in the way we deliver energy.

Blackouts are not unusual in the world. Across the globe, people live in places where energy is unreliable and unavailable. The Qur'an says:

> But squander not (your wealth) in the manner of a spendthrift. (Qur'an 17:26)

In places where the flow of energy is seldom interrupted, like the Western world, we need to start seeing energy as a blessing. You don't squander blessings. The blackout made clear something that Muslims know in our path, or Deen: everything is connected (the principle of *tawhid*), and the actions that we take in one place affect people in another.

To move toward a more balanced system of energy delivery, we need to recognise that our present system is imbalanced in three ways. First, we have an ageing infrastructure. The wires and pipes are getting old! Second, we have an increased demand. Humans are consuming more and more. Third, we are using energy sources that create pollution—like the mountaintop coal removal discussed in chapter 5, 'Energy from Hell'.

We have addressed the need to get a 'smart grid' that would generate data about how people use energy so that changes can be made accordingly. We've also examined the sourcing of energy and the need to move from energy from hell toward energy from heaven. Getting some portion of our energy use off the ageing grid is a greater challenge. In part, it requires that we have the smart grid. At some point, we will need to think about having a less centralized system altogether and opt for smaller, more localised energy delivery.

As an individual, you can begin to imagine your own 'what if the lights went out' moment. How would you handle a blackout? During the 2003 blackout, I thought about how people look to their faith traditions for answers in times of uncertainty and seek solace in meditation or prayer. I wondered what would it look like if during a blackout, all the houses of worship across the Northeast—churches, temples, synagogues, and mosques—were shining beacons of light in a sea of darkness because they were off the grid.

The Power of Intentional Communities

Sometimes the answer to our energy problems is found in a way of life that is completely different from our current lifestyle. You can call it 'going back to nature'. This approach is not for everyone, but living off the beaten path is one in which we, as Muslims, can practise our religion so as to not be part of the system of overconsumption.

In Chiapas, Mexico, there is a Muslim community living completely off the grid. The person who introduced me to these pioneers was Umaya Espinosa, a Muslim woman whose experience has led her to a Green Deen through expressing her faith in concert with her love of the planet and of God, and using the signs (*ayat*) of Allah to guide her toward people who have take their role as stewards (*khalifah*) of the Earth as a central part of their Deen.

Kathy Umaya Espinosa's grandparents were born in Mexico, but Kathy was born in Fullerton, California, the youngest of eight siblings. She enjoyed a very average Christian American upbringing in Los Angeles, where the Espinosa family frequently attended St. John the Evangelist Catholic Church. As immigrants to America, Kathy's family often felt pressures to assimilate, and Kathy and her siblings therefore grew up speaking English.

Kathy first encountered Islam as a college student at San Jose State University, where she met Hana and Tyson, two young Muslims who would become her best friends. To help answer Kathy's questions about Islam, Hana and Tyson gave her a book on Islam and food. This book proved to be a prescient gift. Kathy's father had just passed away from diabetes, and she recalls the doctor saying that diabetes was a 'meat-eating disease'. Kathy reflected on the amount of pork her family, specifically her father, consumed, and reading this book made her want to read more about Islam. She read about the prophets and learned that Muslims believe in Jesus. She wondered, How come the world makes Islam out to be so different?

After 'officially' becoming Muslim, Kathy, now Umaya,[1] began to look for communities that shared her values. As her Muslim identity developed, so did her Mexican identity. She relearned Spanish and travelled to Mexico. In Chiapas, a small town near the Mexican border with Guatemala, Umaya discovered the Alpujarra Muslim community, a functioning Muslim colony. The community operates successful local textile and carpentry businesses and provides Qur'an lessons for its children and youth. Possibly most remarkable, this small community of Muslims lives off the grid.

The Alpujarra Muslim community is a model for anyone interested in a Green Deen, particularly living a life that honours the trust (*amanah*) we have with God to be protectors of the planet. Daily life includes eating fruits and produce from local organic farms. Livestock are used for labour and are maintained in a cruelty-free manner; cows graze freely and eat natural grass. Almost everything—work, school, food—is within walking distance of everyone's home. If automobiles are needed, many families depend on one car. Villagers spin and weave sheep's wool for textiles and garments, such as the *hijab*—the traditional head covering of Muslim women. The textiles are often sold to tourists, the main income source for some families. Doing business locally eliminates the need to import goods. All these practices are local, sustainable, and without exploitation of people, animals, or the planet.

The community has also harnessed solar power. Homes have solar panels made of scrap metal and wooden frames. Water is heated by the sun in buckets placed on the rooftops. One brother has fashioned a solar-heated shower in his home.

Three buckets of water on the rooftop are connected with plastic tubes (made from plastic found in the local market), one of which leads into the home and connects to a showerhead. Solar fruit drying is also a common practice in the Alpujarra community. This is an excellent way to preserve food and is one of the world's oldest agricultural preserving techniques.[2] Sun-drying fruit requires a place with no moisture, thinly sliced fruit, and a safe place to spread the fruit. Some ancient cultures were known to hang fruit slices in sunny spots on tree branches. The Alpujarra community's dependence on sunlight and commitment to living off the grid is impressive and worth emulating.

With 1.4 billion Muslims on this planet, think of the massive impact if we attempted to become smarter about energy, harnessed solar power, and started moving toward off-the-grid lifestyles. We should invest in solar photovoltaics, which turn sunlight into electricity. We should become experts in the next generation of green building design. Our engineers should be skilled in drilling for geothermal heat sources. Our scientists and physicists and venture capitalists should support and develop large-scale wind energy. We must become leading thinkers in biomass, wave energy, hydropower, pumped-storage hydroelectricity, and solar thermal technologies. We should be courageous and bold and strike out to create intentional communities. Or we could at least incorporate small do-it-yourself techniques like fruit drying and solar water heating, all to raise our children to understand the value of living in harmony and balance with the natural world (*mizan*).

With a population of 1.4 billion, high-level thinkers, engineers, scientists, doctors, lawyers, and burgeoning politicians, and Muslims control of much of the world's oil resources can help the whole world move toward a more sustainable and healthy planet. As we move toward justice (*adl*) in how we interact with the Earth, and as we reconnect with the sacred trust (*amanah*) we have with our Creator to be the stewards (*khalifah*) of the Earth, we see something profound. We are the environment (*tawhid*), and in 'going off the grid' we can reconnect with the signs (*ayat*) of the natural world, get our hands in the dirt, test our faculties of intelligence, pray outside, and rise and retire with the movement of the glorious sun and moon as the Creator intended.

This way of living has guided people of all centuries and all places. Now imagine what we could do if we could learn from the thousands of years of history of all our traditions. If we look toward these traditions and see how much guidance they offer on protecting the planet, we could truly, together, offer a light to the world that would not go out.

In what way can you and your community transform some (or all) parts of basic living so that you make no impact on the environment? Could you live off the grid?

Part III Water

We made from water every living thing.
(Qur'an 21:30)

Water is the medium of understanding, faith, and wisdom and a key to the practice of Islam. Prayer opens the heart, and preparing for prayer, physically and spiritually, requires water. As prayer opens your heart, you will be more in tune with the signs of Allah (*ayat*) that are all around us. Water is one of these signs. Whether it is in the gentle mist that cools your lips, or between your toes as you walk barefoot through long grass tipped with morning dew, water is important to how our path of Islam is a faith in concert with protecting and cherishing the planet—a Green Deen.

Water is an integral part of most faith traditions. Most Christian congregations are baptised by being dipped three times in water to signify their birth into a new life in the church. In Judaism, the tradition of the *mikvah,* or ritual bathing, is used to achieve a state of spiritual purity. For Hindus, the Ganges River is considered sacred and is used for spiritual bathing. Some traditional religions have ceremonies that honour the spirits in oceans or in waterfalls.[1] Before 1.4 billion Muslims turn to face their Lord in prayer, they perform *wudu*—the ritual cleansing.

Water is necessary for survival and for the spirit. The Prophet Muhammad (peace be upon him) would take his water in the mornings warm with honey.[2] We sit at the edge of seas, rivers, and ponds and ponder. Water transfixes us with its beauty and frightens us with its awesome powers of destruction.

Water is one of the most constant and reliable signs of God.

Everything is connected (*tawhid*); everything has a relationship with water. Celestial forces connect to water—the tides
are directed by the gravitational pull of the moon. Babies
exist in the watery womb before arriving in the world. Water
behaves in the scripture as it behaves in our lives—it is ubiquitous, flowing in and out of everything.

As in parts I and II, throughout this section we will be
exploring how we can bring the six principles of a Green
Deen to bear on the management of water: understanding
the Oneness of God and His creation (*tawhid*); seeing signs
of God everywhere (*ayat*); being stewards of the Earth (*khalifah*); honouring the trust we have with God (*amanah*); moving
toward justice (*adl*); and living in balance with nature (*mizan*).

I ask you, then: if water is so sacred and integral to all the
paths of the planet, why is it that almost a billion people go
without fresh drinking water every day? If water is so essential
for cleanliness, then why is it that the search for water dominates time that could otherwise be spent on education and the
pursuit of other livelihoods? If water is needed for life, then
why do we keep it from the mouths of those who need it most?

Chapter 9

Water—Essential for Survival

What we know from our Deen, the path or the way of Islam, is that we are not the owners of anything in the universe. This includes a molecule made up of two hydrogen atoms and one oxygen atom: water. The Earth is 70 percent water.[1] The sombre trust that we have with our Creator (*amanah*) to be stewards (*khalifah*) of the Earth means that we will be held accountable for our actions. These actions include those related to water.[2] If the Earth is a mosque, then 70 percent of our mosque is water. Our mosque is oceans, streams, rivers, lakes, springs, and wells. It is our right to benefit from water; indeed, we need it for sheer survival. However, we negate that right if we contaminate, poison, or withhold water from plants, animals, and our fellow humans—all of whom also need water for survival.

Water as a Shared Resource

This chapter advances two main points regarding the distribution of water. First, water should be a community-shared resource. Second, water should be managed by governments who operate justly. The equitable sharing and just managing of water is central to a Green Deen, the path and religion that espouses the Oneness of God and His creation; it is the most basic way to support Oneness (*tawhid*), justice (*adl*), and balance (*mizan*) in this world. We all come from water, we all need water to survive, and we all are responsible for keeping water safe for everyone.

When water is used incorrectly, it becomes a conduit for death instead of life. Just look at the statistics provided by the World Health Organization (WHO). In 2008, WHO reported that 3.6 million people die each year from water-related diseases, and that 84 percent of those deaths are children aged zero to fourteen.[3] Lack of water means not only lack of what your body needs to sustain itself but also lack of sanitation. Eighty-eight percent of diarrhoea cases worldwide are attributable to unsafe water, inadequate sanitation, or insufficient hygiene as a result of lack of access to clean water.[4] The extraction of water in the developing world also takes a large toll on women, who in many countries have to walk an average of six kilometres just to get water.[5] These statistics paint a bleak picture for the world's water situation.

There is no magic pill to address water management issues, but we can look to our faith for guidance. Over fourteen hundred years ago, the first Muslims received divine and prophetic directives regarding water use. Committing harm against any living thing is like committing harm against all of humanity.[6] Restricting access to water is akin to inflicting harm. Doing so has dire consequences: death and disease.

The Prophet Muhammad (peace be upon him) warned his followers of the consequences for withholding water: 'There are three persons whom Allah will not look at on the Day of Resurrection, nor will he purify them and theirs shall be a severe punishment. One of them is a man [who] possessed superfluous water on a way and he withheld it from travellers.'[7] Therefore, to be someone favoured by the Creator, creating access to water for everyone is essential.

I strongly feel that water should be cooperatively owned. It is the tradition of our Deen that water sources such as springs, wells, rivers, lakes, and the like—all signs (*ayat*) of Allah— belong only to Allah and are meant for everyone. God says:

> And We send the winds fertilising, then send down water from the cloud so We give it to you to drink of, nor is it you who store it up. (Qur'an 15:22)

God controls water. It is not ours. Like everything else, we have been given responsibility to cherish it as the gift it is and to take care of it:

> Do you bring it Down (in rain) from the Cloud or do We? Were it Our Will, We could make it salty (and unpalatable): Then why do you not give thanks? (Qur'an 56:69–70)

Water Management

I feel that governments should be responsible for managing water, because the primary role of government is to provide security, and the most basic human need for security is water. Water access for everyone promotes well-being for all. A healthy water network that repairs leaks and modernises ageing systems, that uses new irrigation methods, that recycles waste water, and that thinks long-term will be able to manage water resources and act in the best interests of people and planet.[8]

Islamic history provides examples of managing water in fair

and equitable ways. For instance, the Prophet Muhammad (peace be upon him) spoke of a well that was privately owned by a citizen who was charging a high price for people to use it. The Holy Prophet (peace be upon him) said, 'For anyone who will purchase the Ruma Well and use its water jointly with other Muslims a wonderful place in the Garden of Eden will be prepared.' So the Prophet's companion, Uthman, bought the well and made its use free for the people of Medina.[9] Later, Uthman became one of the caliphs (political leaders) of Islam. He maintained the well so that his constituents would always have access to water.

If you have never been politically active before, this is the moment: now is the time, and water is your cause. Currently, the Clean Water Act is weak at preventing the pollution of water sources. The act needs more teeth to effectively regulate what does and doesn't get dumped into our water. Empowered citizens who make water a priority can compel elected officials to do the same and to take a fresh look at the Clean Water Act.

Anyone can be a part of something as blessed (and necessary) as digging or repairing a well for those in need of water. Everyone can participate in lobbying their local elected officials to invest heavily in public water utilities—building new lines and repairing old ones, fixing old pipes and connecting new ones. All of us should join campaigns to fight the privatisation of water and to stop bottled water companies from creating waste in the name of selling us what is already (or should be) ours.

Turn your Green Deen 'blue' by setting up a water recycling station in your mosque so the water used for *wudu* can also be used to water the plants and grass outside. Install water-saving appliances in your home. Take shorter showers. Never, ever, dump anything into the local water supply. Don't buy bottled water! What we choose to do now is a choice we make for ourselves and for future generations. It is a choice we make on the great blue and green planet we lovingly call home. Remember, our actions related to water, in all its forms, reflect our relationship with the Earth.

Some 97.5% of water on Earth is salty. Around 1 percent of that is brackish groundwater. Some 2.5 percent of the Earth's water is fresh. About two-thirds of that is frozen in ice. That leaves less than 1 percent of the Earth's water supply for us to survive.[10]

How are you going to ensure that this small percentage of water not only lasts, but is available for everyone coexisting on the planet Earth?

Chapter 10

Toxic Waste in Our Water

A Green path, or Deen, recognises that how we manage waste, watts, and food also impacts our water. This chapter looks at industrial practises and how they have mistreated our water systems.

Water is integral to human life, and the way corporations treat water points to the value they place on human life. The Qur'an says:

We made from water every living thing. (Qur'an 21:30)

Yet for over a century, large corporations have used our water sources as their dumping grounds. The effects have lasted for decades and have caused numerous untold deaths.

One of the worst examples is the mercury poisoning of Japan's Minamata Bay. Chisso Corporation, a Japanese chemical company, dumped waste mercury into the bay for decades, denied it, and sat back to watch as the contamination destroyed the local fishing stock and sickened the lives of thousands of residents.

Chisso used mercury as a catalyst to produce a variety of materials. It prospered during post–World War II reconstruction and by 1950 was a dominant force in the fishing town of Minamata, even while it dumped wastewater into the local bay. In the 1950s, mullet, lobster, and shad began disappearing. Dead fish floated and birds dropped dead from the sky. By 1954, patients with impaired nervous systems were coming to the hospital at the Chisso plant. Bodies were racked with convulsions, and newborns showed birth defects. Fishermen and their families were most affected by what came to be called the Minamata disease.[1]

It's not just chemical companies that dump their waste into our water supplies—it's coal companies, food companies, and pretty much any company that uses industrial practices to make and sell its goods. There is, in fact, an entire industry devoted to cleaning up the mess these companies have created in our water systems.

Coal and Water

The processing of coal to produce electricity has negative effects on streams, lakes, and underground water sources. In chapter 5, we looked at how coal is extracted from the ground and, these days, from mountaintops as well. Both of these processes, especially the latter, ruin waterways. The explosions used to blast earth in mountaintop coal removal bury valleys and streams under piles and piles of rubble and ash. According to a November 2009 statement by Mary Anne Hitt, deputy director of the Sierra Club Beyond Coal Campaign, coal companies have already buried close to two thousand miles of Appalachian streams. 'Only swift and decisive action,' says Hitt, 'will protect communities and waterways from mountaintop coal removal.'[2] The Appalachian statistics are but a microcosm of the extraction problems that exist all over the world where precious metals and materials are pulled out of the ground.

Prior to the advent of mountaintop coal removal, West Virginia had some of the cleanest water in the country. Water originating in the mountains would be filtered naturally as it dripped its way down into the valleys and became streams. Today, with the explosion of mountaintops to extract coal, drinking water in mountaintop coal mining regions is contaminated with metals. According to anti-coal organiser Stephanie Tyree, in some West Virginia communities 90 percent of people are drinking contaminated water.[3]

The contamination process begins with the explosion of the mountaintop and continues with the cleaning and processing of the coal. Once the coal has been extracted, it is cleaned with a mixture of chemicals. The resulting by-product, called sludge, is stored in artificial ponds that contain billions of gallons of this toxic and soupy mess. Tyree says, 'One of the West Virginian toxic coal ponds is the largest in the Western Hemisphere, holding some 7.5 billion gallons of sludge.' These toxic dumps are all over the world and seep into our clean and natural water supplies, changing them from safe to very unsafe.

Water is the Achilles' heel of the coal industry, and focusing on water may very well be the only way the destructive practices of the industry will be curbed. 'Water', says Tyree, is the thing that the coal industry cannot win on.' As part of following a Green Deen, you can help protect water by limiting your energy use and by joining the campaigns against mountaintop removal coal mining. Not only is mountaintop coal mining an energy issue, it's a major water issue as well.

Groundwater Contamination

Tauhirah, my youngest sister, is an example of someone living a Green Deen. Mixing her love of Islam and her love of the environment in her career in environmental engineering, she drives around the Northeast in her *hijab* (head scarf), looking for *halal* (in Islam, 'permissible') meals, places to pray, and toxic chemicals.[4]

Tauhirah works for an environmental consulting firm that cleans up groundwater and soil. Her company represents corporate clients, including chemical, pharmaceutical, oil, and gas companies. These companies approach Tauhirah's firm when they've created a mess. Her job is to look for contaminants classified as toxic metal compounds or for heavy metals like arsenic, nickel, cadmium, and zinc. She sees first-hand how the signs (*ayat*) of God in nature are polluted by human action and/or neglect. She also searches for volatiles, semivolatiles, pesticides, and polychlorinated biphenyls (PCBs) — contaminants for which the Environmental Protection Agency (EPA) has set standards for -safe- limits.

The sites that Tauhirah visits often have contaminated groundwater. Groundwater — water located directly beneath the surface of the ground — has agricultural and municipal uses. Contamination can occur from a spill or through a leak from an underground toxic waste storage tank. Some sites are where a company dumped hazardous waste — sometimes as long as thirty years ago — and covered it up with a landfill, thinking this would solve the problem. Tauhirah recalls being at a site to sample the streams, groundwater, and sediment. The site was beautiful, covered with trees and grass. Soon enough, however, she realised she was standing atop a landfill. With a little kick of dirt, she began to see remnants of old tyres, syringes, and plastics. As she put it, 'It was like you would open up the ground and see all this garbage poured into the wounds of the Earth.' In these instances, not only is groundwater toxic, it's been covered over and is potentially filled with microorganisms, disinfectants, disinfection by-products, inorganic chemicals, and radionuclides—all of which the EPA has established standards and tests for.[5] With all these dangerous contaminants in the water, we can see that the delicate balance (*mizan*) of nature is in peril.

Tauhirah's Green Deen takes the form of environmental protection. She is on the front lines of an ecological struggle that tests her faith and passion for justice (*adl*) every day. When asked if she's ever sick of her job, she says no. It reminds her of her responsibility to protect the planet (*khalifah*)—or, more accurately, her responsibility to reverse the damage that has already been done to the planet. Tauhirah takes the trust (*amanah*) she has with God seriously and wholeheartedly, and treks every day trying to reverse the course of over one hundred years of industrial process—one step at a time.

Bottles Make Bad Water

Bottles themselves become waste as we discard them, but bottling processes also create toxic waste in our water supplies. Coca-Cola has been in trouble around the world for its purported toxic waste dumping practices, especially in India, where Coca-Cola factories have allegedly been polluting water for decades.

According to protestors, to create Coca-Cola, the company draws water from local groundwater. In addition, the process of production, bottling, and shipping creates sludge that is dumped back into the land. In one reported incidence, Coke was selling its solid waste as fertiliser.[6] The Coca-Cola Company has been accused not only of polluting land and water but also of creating water shortages in the Indian communities surrounding its plants.[7]

Bottled water is just water that has become a $400 billion global industry known as 'Blue Gold'. Coca-Cola is the manufacturer of Dasani bottled water, Pepsi makes Aquafina, and of course there's Evian, Poland Spring, and Ice Mountain.[8] A 20-ounce bottle of water might cost around $1. That's 5 cents per ounce. There are 128 ounces in a gallon, so if you buy your water in 20-ounce bottles, you could be paying $6.40 per gallon for it. According to the American Water Works Association, most municipal water costs less than 1 cent per gallon. Bottled water is big business, and it's fooling millions of us.

Most bottled water is simply filtered tap water marketed to be safer and cleaner. In 2007, PepsiCo was forced to admit that its best-selling Aquafina bottled water is nothing more than tap water. Today Aquafina is still tap water. Pepsi simply changed the label to indicate that the water comes from a public source.[9] This is one way of knowing that here in America our public water is relatively safe! In fact, it might be safer than some bottled waters. According to the National Resources Defense Council, in a scientific study in which more than a thousand bottles of 103 brands of water were tested, about one-third of the bottles contained 'significant contamination' (that is, levels of chemical or bacterial contaminants exceeding those allowed under a state or industry standard or guideline) from synthetic organic chemicals, bacteria, and arsenic.[10] In 2004, Coca-Cola had to withdraw Dasani bottled water from United Kingdom stores because some samples were found to contain elevated amounts of bromate, a potentially harmful chemical.[11]

Our obsession with bottled water is taking our attention away from improving and protecting our municipal water systems. Many scholars have argued that, in Islam, selling water is actually an unlawful practice. In the Shariah,[12] there is a stipulation that does not allow one to attach a cost to water for profit.[13] Living a Green Deen is, therefore, not consistent with selling (and buying) bottled water. The more bottled water we buy, the more waste we create and the more we empower corporations to sell what is readily available in our taps. Furthermore, instead of empowering companies to bottle and sell what our municipalities provide, we should be pressuring our governments to improve water quality standards.

Improving Water Quality Standards

The Clean Air Act prevents companies from spewing toxic chemicals into the atmosphere, but the Clean Water Act needs strengthening to reach this same standard. Currently, the Clean Water Act has too many loopholes that prevent the EPA from enforcing it appropriately. For example, only water that is 'navigable', or what an average citizen would consider a waterway, is protected under the act.[14] Therefore, if a company can prove that a small stream or bit of groundwater is not 'navigable', they currently have the right to dump their waste in it.[15] The problem with this loophole is that dumping into small sources has large consequences from leaks and spills. Since we know from our principal of Oneness (*tawhid*) that

everything is connected, the negative consequences hurt not
only some of us—but all of us.

We can do a few simple things to mitigate the harm
humans cause to water. First, we need to be mindful of waste.
Remember that Allah has said in the Qur'an:

> But waste not by excess, for Allah loves not the wasters.
> (Qur'an 7:31)

By treating the natural world as though it were our dumping
ground, we risk disturbing the delicate balance (*mizan*) that
exists in nature. Anything packaged will generate physical
waste and most likely also toxic waste that eventually finds its
way into the water system. We should, therefore, as a part of
our Green Deen, try to limit the amount of packaged goods
we purchase, especially bottled water! Second, we should
speak out against injustice. Join campaigns against corporations that dump toxic wastes into water sources. Urge the
government to strengthen its regulations to prevent, and stop,
such destructive actions.

A Green Deen is about upholding justice to the planet and
its people (*adl*). The Prophet Muhammad (peace be upon
him) said: 'Whoever among you sees an evil action, let him
change it with his hand [by taking action]; if he cannot, then
with his tongue [by speaking out]; and if he cannot, then with
his heart [by hating it and feeling that it is wrong]—and that
is the weakest of faith.'[16] The Prophet Muhammad (peace be
upon him) was urging humanity to take action and speak out,
and at the very least, recognise in our hearts when something
is wrong.

Every day we are part of the glorious cycle of the Earth that
includes the moon, the clouds, and ourselves. The moon plays

a role in the movement of water on Earth, as it determines the tides of the bodies of water. As water cycles from clouds to rain and snow, in streams and rivers it flows down from mountains, eventually arriving where we need it most: at the land we cultivate and in our bodies. Let's use the lessons of a Green Deen to make sure that we do not contribute to the contamination of water. Our health depends on it.

One of the core lies of the age is that we can do nothing to change the world around us, that this is 'just the way things are.' In this chapter we have seen that bottled water is often just tap water and an excuse for people to make money. It has been claimed by advocates and activists worldwide that the production of bottled beverages has limited the water access surrounding the factories that produce these beverages. We have also seen that industrial practices have made people sick from dumping waste into areas that people use to harvest fish.

Given all that, and with the BP oil spill in the Gulf of Mexico fresh in your mind, here's a question for you: Knowing what you now know, can you envision a world in which everyone has access to clean and free drinking water?

Chapter 11

The Wonderful World of Wudu

Muslims have a special relationship with water. It is one of the great signs (*ayat*) of God in nature, and it has been mentioned specifically in the verses of the Qur'an. Water is indeed a sign of Allah that is everywhere in one of its many forms. For everyday Muslims, water is nothing more than an expression of the covenant, or trust (*amanah*), we have with God, for with it we ritually purify ourselves to begin each act of worship. The Prophet Muhammad (peace be upon him) said that 'cleanliness is half of faith.'

For Muslims, cleanliness begins with the practice of bathing and ablution, or *wudu,* the ritual cleansing before each prayer. We make wudu every day, sometimes five times a day. Water is essential for this most important ritual, but we can also make wudu part of our green, eco-conscious way of living our Deen, the path of Islam, by being conscious of how we use this most precious gift.

The Qur'an gives us the origin and power of water:

He sends down water from the skies, and the channels flow, each according to its measure. (Qur'an 13:17)

God also tells us that water will replenish us. He says:

> [We] sent down rain from the heavens; and brought forth
> therewith fruits for your sustenance. (Qur'an 2:22)

Our Creator will provide for us, but we cannot take this provision for granted.

Currently in the United States, each person may use as much as 570 litres of water each day for drinking, cleaning, and the like. Meanwhile, more than a billion people in the world do not have access to clean and safe drinking water.[1] In this chapter, I examine our relationship to water and present some practical steps we can take to green our Deen while making wudu.

Ablution

All three traditional monotheistic faiths have some form of ablution, or ritual cleansing. Christianity has baptism, Judaism has *netilat yadayim* (hand washing), and Islam has wudu.[2]

The practice of wudu is derived from the Qur'an, which says:

> O you who believe! When you prepare for prayer, wash
> your faces, and your hands (and arms) to the elbows; rub
> your heads (with water); and (wash) your feet to the ankles.
> (Qur'an 5:6)

This is the basic structure of wudu. Further details of completing wudu are derived from the sayings (the hadith) and the actions (the sunnah) of the Prophet Muhammad (peace be upon him).

The idea of wudu is to cleanse yourself of worldly things before entering the spiritual world through prayer. Each day your goal is to exercise your faith, to move toward justice (*adl*), and to maintain the balance (*mizan*) that God has created. You begin wudu by washing your hands three times—for what you did with those hands. Next you rinse your mouth three times— for what you said. Then you rinse your nose three times—to cleanse yourself of any acts of arrogance. Next you wash your eyes and face—so that you shine to the angels that gather around for prayer. Finally, you wash each arm up to the elbow three times, then your ears, over your head, your neck, and each foot.

For 1.4 billion Muslims, wudu is an obligatory cleanse before each of the obligatory five daily prayers and before reading the Qur'an in Arabic. It is also a good state to be in, as it makes us more spiritually aware and tuned in to the Oneness of all creation (*tawhid*) around us. Being in a state of wudu means that at any moment we can bend our knees in prayer, and it allows us the blessing of turning even a walk to the grocery store, or a drive to the office, to be an opportunity for a deeper connection to our role as a stewards (*khalifah*) and representatives of Allah on the Earth.

A person with a Green Deen is mindful of the amount of water used during wudu. Although wudu is an essential and vital part of Islamic practice, the Prophet Muhammad (peace be upon him) taught thriftiness with water. He warned against wasting water when doing wudu, even if one lives near a river.[3] Today, however, many of us tend to forget this 'green' practice of the Holy Prophet (peace be upon him). To be perfectly honest, I've seen my fellow Muslims go a little overboard with wudu—making it almost a mini shower. We can, and should, look to find a natural place of balance (*mizan*) with what is necessary to conduct the cleanse and what we can do to emulate the Messenger of Allah (peace be upon him) in not wasting water just for religious purposes.

Here in the United States, we often need to make wudu outside our home or mosque. Sometimes we are travelling across the country and have to stop at a highway rest stop, or we are at a hotel or in the crowded bathroom of an office. Each place presents different challenges; what should be constant is our thriftiness of use. At home, we have towels and a bathtub that can make the process easier, and mosques have created wudu-friendly sinks that are low to the ground. However, the bathroom in your office building is probably not too wudu-friendly. Not only is taking a mini shower there contradictory to a Green Deen, it's bad manners to leave the public restroom soaked—it is, among other things, unclean and dangerous.

A Green Deen asks us to be more mindful of our water usage and to be respectful of those around us who may or may not understand the rituals of our faith. We need to set a solid example for the management of all the resources the Almighty has provided. It is a blessing of our tradition to be so connected to water.

What's Your Wudu Number?

To green our wudu, we need to begin by figuring out how much water we're now using for wudu—our 'wudu number'.[4] How can we do this? Interestingly, in the United States, this question hasn't been explored in depth yet, so I'm going to give it a shot—of course, with a little help from the scores of people I have asked this question at conferences and talks across the country.

If you use running water and a sink to do ablution, you can find your wudu number in three simple steps. To make this process the easiest, try making wudu in the bathtub so you can measure what you use—or rather, waste!

1. Find a timer and start it when you begin doing wudu. Stop the timer when you're done.
2. Get a bucket and place it under the tap. Turn on the tap at the same force you used in doing your wudu, and keep the water running for the same amount of time that it took you to do your wudu.
3. Use a measuring cup to measure the amount of water in the bucket. This is your wudu number. It may not be perfect, but it's a start. Having a number of some kind can help you determine a goal for reducing that number.

As part of greening your mosque, you can also determine the wudu number of the entire community. Here's how I think this could be done:

1. Pick an average Friday at your mosque to run the experiment. (Note: You will not want to do this experiment on a Friday when people are gathered for a meal and much water is being used in meal preparation and cleanup.)
2. Check the water meter early in the morning and record the reading.
3. Recruit volunteers to count the number of people who do wudu throughout the day.
4. Right before the mosque closes, record the reading on the water meter. The difference between the morning and the

evening readings gives the amount of water used that day in the mosque.

5. Assuming that the majority of the water used goes toward wudu, this will be the wudu number for that day for that community. Dividing the difference in the meter readings by the number of people who did wudu gives the approximate wudu number for each person.

For a more accurate number, run the experiment every Friday for three months and take an average. Or try to do the experiment every day for a few consecutive months for an even stronger number. Either way, you will have a number to work with and can even make a community challenge out of it.

The ADAMS Center Mosque outside of Washington, DC, home to the DC Green Muslims—mentioned in chapters 3 and 4—has pledged to reduce its energy and water consumption by 10 percent.[5] What if all the mosques in the country aimed to reduce their wudu numbers by 10 percent? Mosques could post the water meter readings on a big chart and challenge the community to use less water when making wudu. Attaching a dollar amount to the water usage and monitoring the wudu number by the decrease in water bills could serve as an additional motivator to reduce the mosque's water use.

Knowing our wudu number is important for reducing our water usage, as it is, like any piece of data, a tool that can be used to help us make decisions. Perhaps we are not wasting that much water after all, or maybe, we use more or less at different times of day. Most important, knowing your wudu number will help you to understand your relationship to the planet.

We live in a society that uses data to make just about every decision. We use our knowledge of sports statistics to play fantasy football, fantasy basketball, and fantasy baseball and make decisions about which team members to keep and which ones to get rid of for the ideal roster. In our commute, we calculate the best time to leave our house to minimise the amount of traffic we encounter or to make certain we make it to the bus or train station at the right time. We analyse data every day when we do a scan of the weather, comparing it to the same time last year.

The government uses the census to determine how many people live in a community, how many congressional seats that community gets, and, ultimately, how much funding that community will receive for a variety of services. Having a baseline wudu number can help you manage your water usage and help our communities become more conscious of their overall water use. As you begin to know your personal wudu number, you may find that you're also becoming more mindful of your overall consumption in every aspect of your life.

Water-Saving Steps You Can Take

A Malaysian company has developed an automated water-dispensing machine that uses sensors to conserve water during wudu. Invented by AACE Technologies, the machine uses only 1.3 litres (0.3 gallons). 'During the Hajj, 2 million people use approximately 50 million litres of water per day. If they introduce this machine, they are saving nearly 40 million litres per day', said AACE chairman Anthony Gomez.[6] This company's wudu machines are expensive, about $3,000 to $4,000 each, but still they point to the reality that we need to transform the way we think about water and perform wudu differently.

There are three easy things you can do to reduce your water use and to live a Green Deen in respect to water. Most of us are already familiar with these suggestions, and we may already be following them—but we can always do better!

1. *Take shorter showers!* Yes, this may be hard for many of us, but it's very important.
2. *Turn off the tap when you're brushing your teeth.* There is no reason to have the water on while going up and down and round and round on those pearly whites.
3. *Use cold water instead of hot while doing the laundry.* Hot water requires energy for heating and is not necessary for clothes washing.

These are three very simple things that will help us become better managers of the most critical substance on Earth—water.

So, what is your wudu number, and how can you lower it?

Part IV Food

O Children of Adam! Wear your beautiful apparel at every time and place of prayer: eat and drink: but waste not by excess, for Allah loves not the wasters.

(Qur'an 7:31)

I am a foodie. As I write this I am staring at a ripe mango, anxious to bite into it. My mother taught me to be a food-conscious individual. She taught us to read the labels on all foods in the grocery store. If we couldn't pronounce the ingredients, we couldn't buy the product. We had lunches filled with raw broccoli and tuna—and we loved it. Other kids had more typical American lunches that included ham, sugary juices, and cookies, but we were not impressed. The more processed the food, the less we were interested in it.

More than two decades have passed since those days of learning how to eat healthily, but to this day, what I choose to eat is at the core of my Green Deen—the path I have chosen to be mindful of the consequences that my actions have on the planet and its animals, plants, and people. In regard to food, this is a path that my ancestors walked even if they were not Muslim by name. They were African, Cherokee, Arapahoe, Sioux.

The choices we make around food are intertwined with all six principles of a Green Deen. From where our food comes from to what the food is, we need to make better choices. Earlier we talked about the signs of God in the natural world. These signs (*ayat*) are how the food we eat exists in its natural state. An apple dangling from a tree, a berry bouncing on a bush, a chicken on a free-range farm, and a fish in a murky lake all exist in harmonious balance (*mizan*) with the rest of the natural world. We are part of this cycle. As the stewards (*khalifah*) of the Earth, we make choices every day to nourish ourselves so that we can praise God with all of our strength. To eat, we must take from the bounty of the Earth's plants and animals. Our Deen, or path, dictates we do so while mindful of the trust (*amanah*) we have with God to maintain the balance (*mizan*) and do justice (*adl*) in our dealings with animals, plants, and people.

Thousands of years ago, Allah gave us the template for healthy eating: organic, free-range *halal,* or permissible, foods. By opting for locally grown seasonal produce and by using only meat from pasture-raised, grass-fed, and humanely treated livestock, we move away from the injustice of the factory farm system and toward practices that reflect the principle of justice (*adl*). We are what we eat, just as we are connected to everything in the universe because of the Oneness of God and His creation (*tawhid*).

Allah reminds us in *ayah* after *ayah* of the bounty in creation. For example, Surah Rahman, a sublime chapter of the Qur'an clearly states that God has given His creation bounty on Earth:

> Then which of the favours of your Lord will you deny?
> (Qur'an 55:13)

It is in this wonderful bounty that we have the greatest opportunity to showcase the best of our Deen, protecting the planet while nourishing ourselves and our families with food that will aid us in our praise of God. As New Testament scholar Hal Taussig of Union Theological Seminary has noted, it was the early Christians who would gather round for communal meals who helped to secure mealtime as family time.[1] There is nothing better than eating healthy and wholesome food that has not exploited anyone or anything—together with people you love.

So much could be written about food! Food is where the management of water, waste, and energy intersect to provide nourishment for our minds, bodies, and souls. It would be difficult to capture everything we need to know about eating healthily. The basic principles of our path, our Deen, look past all the fad diets and exercise routines to provide a simple and straightforward message that takes us back to the first human feeling the first pangs of hunger. The principles require us to know where our food comes from and to place a premium on wholesome, ethical food sources. This section is perhaps the most dynamic of the book because it is where the 'rubber meets the road', where theory and action combine, and where the committed and distributed efforts by small groups of people all over the country are starting to align into a Green Deen food movement that is, as Yasir Syeed says, 'a profound reject of the materialistic philosophy . . . the most intimate way we react in the world.'[2]

Think about all the effort—by nature and by humans—that goes into the food that ends up in our homes. How long does it take for a seed to grow into a tree, for a tree to bear fruit, for the fruit to be harvested and make its way into your home?

Chapter 12

Feeding Your Family

This chapter is about choices we can make to live a Green Deen by bringing the best possible food to our table. It's not easy being parents. We must make many important decisions that affect our family—for instance, where to live and where to send our children to school. Another important decision involves food. Finding healthy, affordable, and convenient food is a challenge for many families. Finding and preparing food that is also consistent with living a Green Deen is an even greater challenge, but there are Muslims who have met this challenge head-on. In this chapter, I'll show you how they've done it.

Factory Farming

First, before getting to stories of Muslims who are living a Green Deen in relation to food, I need to give you some background on what is wrong with most of the food that is easily available to us, especially with regard to meat. Today, most of the meat sold in supermarkets and served in restaurants, especially fast-food restaurants, is raised in what are called factory

'farms', also known as concentrated animal feeding operations, or CAFOs. Here huge numbers of animals are crowded
together in inhumane conditions, pumped with pharmaceu-
ticals to promote growth as rapidly as possible, and slaughtered on assembly 'killing lines'—all for the sake of produc-
ing as much meat as quickly as possible, with as much profit
as possible. When food production is strictly a business with
the sole purpose of making profit, it will never provide high-
quality food that is also mindful of the planet.

The film *Food, Inc.,* shows how animals are treated in factory farms and is a must-see exposé of the factory farming
industry. Cattle are crowded into huge feedlots and left to
stand in their own faeces. Worst of all, they are fed a grain
diet—because it's cheap and easy. Cows are grass-eating animals. Their teeth, their digestive system, and their entire
body are not created to eat corn. The industry also disre-
spects chickens. Thousands of chickens are packed into dirty
chicken houses without natural light. They are fed steroids
and arsenic compounds to promote growth and are bred to
have disproportionately large breasts. These genetically and
pharmaceutically manipulated chickens grow in dramatically less time than do naturally raised chickens and are often
unable to walk more than a few steps because their legs cannot support their weight. Faster-growing and fatter chickens
are cheap to create and great to sell, especially since America's
obsession with white breast meat has increased.

The factory farming industry treats animals the same way
economic systems treat human beings—as units of production. In Islam we are commanded to treat animals with much
more respect, for they are part of God's creation, which we
have sworn to protect. Remember, everything is connected in

the Oneness (*tawhid*) of Allah and His creation. Is this how we want to treat the food that we will put into our bodies?

With millions of Muslims in the United States having a typically American appetite for meat, it seems inevitable that Muslims will either have to interact with the larger food system or create their own to provide *halal* (permissible) food. To determine the status of the *halal* industry, a group called the Halal Advocates of America was formed in 2008,[1] led by American-born and South African–trained Mufti Shaykh Abdullah Nana, a young, bearded, slightly built, and calmly spoken scholar who resides in California. Shaykh Abdullah began learning about *halal* slaughtering by going to slaughterhouses with trained experts in South Africa. When he came back to the United States, he was concerned with the integrity of the *halal* standard and visited thirty-five slaughterhouses in over thirteen states. Since all of U.S. meat does not come from the United States, he also visited slaughterhouses in the United Kingdom, Canada, and New Zealand. The point of his research, he said, was that 'there is a need for first hand verification of *halal* practices.'

In a recent lecture, Shaykh Abdullah talked about the various forms of inadequate certification of *halal* meat, such as 'drive-by', in which a shaykh drives by and reads a prayer as he passes by the slaughterhouse. In some instances, Shaykh Abdullah observed so-called *halal* meat being slaughtered with the same machine and knife used in slaughtering pork (which is forbidden in Islam and Judaism), and other instances in which the basic requirements, according to the sunnah— the practice of the Prophet (peace be upon him)—were not followed. In some cases, the proper cuts were not performed. According to the shaykh's research, 50 percent of Muslims in

America are eating questionable and doubtful *halal* meats.[2] So what is the way forward?

The Deen, the path, of Islam has had a solution to this problem for close to fourteen hundred years. *Halal* meat must be slaughtered in a way in which the appropriate vessels are cut, and the blessing 'Bismillah Allahu Akbar' ('In the name of God, God is Great') must be recited audibly. The next step in determining whether meat is truly *halal* is to know how the animal was raised and how it was processed and distributed. Shaykh Abdullah identifies issues to look for in a slaughter-house, such as how the animals are stunned prior to being killed and the contamination of *halal* meat in the processing.

Vegetarian Muslims

Some Muslims are vegetarian, abstaining from animal or flesh foods, or vegan, additionally avoiding dairy and eggs, as well as fur, leather, wool, down, and cosmetics or chemical products tested on animals,[3] specifically because of the harm done to animals in the factory farming industry. However, it's also possible to live a Green Deen and still eat meat—*halal,* organic, free-range meat. Following are two stories of Muslim families: one that has chosen a vegan path, and one that has chosen the path of organic, free-range *halal* meat.

The Vegan Way

Zachary Twist, whom I first encountered when he was the operations director for Zaytuna College while I studied Arabic there, is a convert to Islam who was a vegan even before becoming a Muslim.[4] He was raised in a household immersed in nonprofit social activism and, as he shared, 'concern for the global human family.' He was taught Green Deen principles by his parents before he was Muslim. They raised him to be deeply conscious of his impact on the people and planet around him—a real steward (*khalifah*) in training. As a young teen, Zachary became the family voice for environmental advocacy, a path that was also developed by formative experiences immersed in the signs of God (*ayat*) mountain biking in the woods —adventures he now shares with his family.

Zachary recalls becoming vegan as a young person after learning about the factory farming industry. He remembers hearing the KRS-One song 'Beef', which outlined the horrors of factory farming and the pain that animals endure all in the name of profit making. He dropped meat from his diet and, eventually, all dairy products as well. Soon he noticed a shift in his mental state and also began exploring his spiritual state.

When Zachary became Muslim, he retained his vegan lifestyle but faced considerable social pressure to eat meat at Muslim gatherings and Eid celebrations. Nevertheless, he remained grounded in the principles of justice (*adl*) and balance (*mizan*), feeling that injustice to animals was not worth his eating meat. Furthermore, he felt strongly about maintaining a balance in his diet. For this, meat was also unnecessary. His relationship with Allah did not depend on eating meat. In fact, he felt that there was no compatibility between the Muslim lifestyle and the factory farming industry. His Muslim brethren questioned his choice to not eat meat at all: 'How can you make what's *halal* (permissible) *haram* (impermissible) for you?' Zachary responded, 'If you do not like something, why be forced to eat it?'

Today Zachary is a husband and father who is committed to

living a Green Deen in all aspects of his life. He and his family maintain a vegan lifestyle and live in Fremont, California, where they have relatively easy access to a variety of farmers' markets that sell fresh, organically grown, exploitation-free fruits and vegetables. Zachary and his wife also decided that home schooling was the ideal path for their young children, whom they wanted to have a strong Islamic foundation before entering the large, secular environment of a public school. Similarly, Zachary is committed to incorporating the Islamic principles of justice and balance in his work and is now learning about building and expanding sustainable businesses while earning a master's degree in business administration. He also remains active as a donor, member, and volunteer in the Sierra Club, the Nature Conservancy, the Pachamama Alliance, YES (Youth for Environmental Sanity), and the Rainforest Action Network.

'My central motivation for all of this, including my diet choices', Zachary stresses, 'is simply treading lightly on the Earth. I concluded at one point in my life that if I can minimize the degradation and suffering caused by my lifestyle, without an excessive amount of cost or inconvenience, why shouldn't I? To me, treading lightly is an Islamic precept.' He cites an *ayah,* or verse, from the Qur'an:

> And the servants of the All-Merciful are they who walk on the earth gently (*hawnan*). (Qur'an 25:63)

'Holy Chicken'

Labinsky Roach and Ridwan Falah are a young interracial Muslim couple who have prioritised food in their lives.[5]

Labinsky is from the Dominican Republic and comes from a strong tradition of eating wholesome foods. She became Muslim, breaking away from her Christian roots, on her own accord. Her husband, Ridwan, is from Indonesia, a place where fresh and organic food was readily available. They have two young sons, Nuh and Ayub—Arabic names for the prophets Noah and Job—and live in Manhattan's Lower East Side.

The Indonesia Ridwan described to me sounded lovely. His family could get food they trusted from the local market and supermarket, and they could even slaughter their own meat at nearby farms whenever they wanted. They didn't have to worry about whether the animals were raised properly, and because they did the slaughter themselves, they didn't have to worry about whether the meat was *halal*. They ate plenty of fish and vegetables.

In Indonesia, healthy food was everywhere, so when Ridwan's family emigrated to New York, they continued to eat freely whatever was readily available. They had lots of McDonald's and fast-food Chinese and Korean food. Fruits and vegetables became a distant memory. Because in Indonesia the *halal* nature of meat was taken for granted, in America Ridwan's family didn't give importance to finding meat that was *halal*.

Then, as Ridwan prepared to graduate from high school, his family went through a spiritual transformation from being culturally Muslim to becoming devout Muslims. Their Deen permeated all aspects of their lives, including the food they chose to eat, and they decided to make a healthy *halal* diet a priority.

Labinsky, Ridwan's wife, learned early in her life the value of eating wholesome foods. In the Dominican Republic, a small Caribbean country sharing the island of Hispaniola with Haiti, she regularly bought meat at a butcher's shop— never at a supermarket. For a short time after emigrating to America, her family lived in Allentown, Pennsylvania, where they raised their own chickens, giving Labinsky a deep understanding of how food gets from the farm to the table. Her family did not stay in Pennsylvania long. Labinksy became Muslim while still in high school in New York City and strengthened her Deen while attending Russell Sage College in Troy, New York. She shifted her already wholesome diet to a *halal* one.

Labinsky and Ridwan are trained educators who combine their Deen and their passion for social justice in making food choices. Their income is limited, and with two young sons, they need to make strategic choices about what to feed their growing family. They first decided they would eat only meat from a Muslim butcher. Then, after learning about and being horrified by the practices of the factory farming industry, they evolved into eating *halal* meat that is pasture raised, grass fed, and free of growth hormones and antibiotics. Wanting also to transform how they eat at restaurants, they decided to select only vegetarian or seafood dishes.

Ridwan and Labinsky are also looking for other Muslim families interested in making a community-supported agriculture (CSA) arrangement with a local farm to supply them with *halal*, organic, free-range meat. They want to be able to trust the person doing the slaughtering and to know that the animal has lived a good life. Their current options are Norwich Meadows Farm in upstate New York, whose farmers often come to the city and sell at farmers' markets, and Green Dhabihah, which can be found online. Both are a bit pricey. Chapter 15, 'Green Dhabihah', discusses the benefits and challenges of eating meat that is double-certified as *halal* and organic. For the moment, Labinsky and Ridwan are trying to figure out how to make more space in their freezer to store their *halal* organic meat purchased in bulk.

Can We Afford to Eat Organic and *Halal*?

Buying organic and *halal* meat can be affordable. Once when I was giving a lecture at Ohio State University, a young man from the Muslim Students' Association asked me whether it was financially feasible to make the shift to organic and *halal*. He was concerned that if the large producers do not make this shift, such a change will never take place, because the large producers have all the money and all the means of production. What he forgot is that we, the consumers, actually hold the power. We can demand certain standards in our food system. When demand patterns change, so will the supply patterns. Simple economics of supply and demand can fall in line with our Deen and not just benefit the producers. The economics of supply and demand can, if applied correctly, also benefit the whole planet.

This understanding is critical to a Green Deen. Our current consumerist ways have left us disconnected from our food—we are mostly ignorant of where it lives and grows before it arrives at our table. If we could be more conscious of our food's life—its beginning and end—perhaps we would be more careful about what we eat.

As I travel the country meeting with different communities of Muslims, I often try to talk about living a Green Deen as it relates to food. However, I find that many communities face challenges in doing so. Cost is one: factory-farmed meat and other foods are less expensive than organic, grass-fed, freely grazed meat and other organic foods. Culture is another: serving meat at gatherings is a sign of wealth and hospitality. We need, I think, an Islamic imperative to avoid factory-farmed meat and nonorganic food. But where can we find one?

In researching this book, I was told by numerous scholars that the Prophet Muhammad (peace be upon him) ate meat only once in a while, and particularly when it was served to him. Meat was a part of his diet, but it surely was not the centrepiece of it. Perhaps this is something from the Islamic tradition that we have forgotten. Perhaps meat is not supposed to be an every-meal or even an everyday part of our diet!

Education is part of the process. By learning about the factory farming industry—that its main goal is to make money, not to feed our families—we can begin to move toward justice (*adl*) by limiting the amount of meat we eat. We can go even further by opting to buy our meat from *halal,* organic, free-range sources. My wife and I recently married and want to be as intentional as possible in the food choices we make. We decided that we would choose to eat mostly vegetarian unless we could find meat that was grass fed and humanely treated, and—of course—*halal.*

We are still the children of our parents, however, and when we are around our elders we eat what they provide. But we also take these mealtimes as a teachable moment. We do not gorge on the food provided, and we do our best to steer the conversation to what we can know about, and how much we can control, how what we eat is raised, cultivated, and brought to our table. We can become more involved in raising and growing our own food—something, as you will see in the next chapter, we can do in our own backyard, or even if we live in a small urban apartment.

My wife and I eat simple meals at home most of the time. Sometimes we eat sushi, never fast food, and for lunch we like leftovers and maybe a local sandwich—humus or tuna. And when it comes to meat, we like to ask people: Do you know the farm where this meat came from? Have you asked your butcher? If so, ask to be taken to the farm where they get their *halal* meat. Do *you* know where your *halal* meat comes from?

Chapter 13

Urban and Suburban Food Gardens

Growing your own food—whether you live in an urban, a suburban, or a rural area—can be a liberating process. When you grow your own food, the connections you make to the planet are tangible. During World Wars I and II, Americans were encouraged to start small gardens called 'Victory Gardens'. These gardens were designed to help provide food for citizens during the war since many agricultural workers had been drafted.[1] We can adapt this approach to fit our present times, when people are looking for healthy organic food at low cost.

Suburban Backyard Food Gardens

Some of the best spaces for growing food happen to be in the suburbs. Take, for example, a family in Brookfield, Wisconsin, a suburb of Milwaukee. It's a nice town with nice people. Some of these nice people are the Ashrafs—the family of my wife, Fatima. They fit the profile the Pew and Gallup polls use to characterise the Muslim American community—well educated, middle-class, and mainstream. They also maintain a Green Deen, living as stewards (*khalifah*) of the Earth and cultivating the land available to them by keeping a backyard garden.

Their garden is as integral to their identity as is their love of football. Tailgating does not involve alcohol because they are Muslims, but they sure can grill like nobody else. They are God fearing and environment loving. As a child, Fatima would stand next to her mother as she prayed five times a day. After Mom had finished praying, she would stay sitting on the prayer rug, teaching Fatima the Arabic alphabet so she would be fluent in the language of the Qur'an. The garden exists as a result of Mom's dedication to her way of life, her religion, her Deen. Fatima's mother believes that God provided soil, seed, and water to be used for good. The religion of Islam tells us that we can see the signs (*ayat*) of Allah all around us; they are ever-present in nature. As dictated to me by Mom herself, her garden is filled with *tamatay* (tomatoes), *pudina* (mint), *phallee* (beans), *behndi* (okra), *laysan* (garlic), *adrak* (ginger), and *baigun* (eggplant). It doesn't stop there. In the different seasons, the Ashrafs' garden also boasts an assortment of peppers and a variety of fruits, including watermelon, pears, apples, apricots, peaches, and a cherry tree that admittedly does not grow many cherries.

The fruits and vegetables of the Ashrafs' garden are used to feed family and friends. The house is always abuzz with visitors waiting for the latest, greatest meal made from produce fresh from the backyard. Don't even think about wasting anything—if you don't finish your entire plate, you first get scolded by the elders and then get sent out to the backyard compost pile with the remains. I used to be afraid of suburbs—

large spaces of arable land turned into strip malls and artificially fed, impeccably green manicured lawns. Thankfully, my wife's family has shattered this image.

Another midwestern gardening Muslim recently caught my attention. His name is Dr. Walid Al-Ghoul, and he lives in Lombard, Illinois. His 'back home' is Palestine, where he learned planting from his mother, who raised him learning how to grow guava, lemons, limes, olives, figs, roses, and jasmine. Since the early 1990s, when he lived in Chapel Hill, North Carolina, Dr. Al-Ghoul has cultivated the soil with his sturdy earthen hands and a soft touch. Today he has two kinds of gardens. One is for common vegetables and herbs. The other is where he plants fruit trees and grapes as a *sadaqa jareyah* (ceaseless charity) for loved ones who have passed away.

City Gardens

The Ashrafs' suburban garden has also made its way into the urban centre that is Brooklyn, New York. In her most recent visit, Fatima's mother brought us some seeds. Using string, old milk jugs, and potting soil from the nearby organic grocery store, Mom created a garden of red and white onions and mint in the kitchen of our tiny Brooklyn apartment. She insisted that someone writing a book called *Green Deen* must have a kitchen garden, no matter how small. It is really nothing special, just a planter that can fit on the window sill, but it's still a garden.

Cities, though crowded and lacking the backyard space of suburban homes, can still be places where people grow their own food. This is the idea behind urban gardening. In a time when parts of our cities are 'food deserts' where people do not have access to wholesome, healthy fresh foods, something needs to be done. According to the New York City Department of City Planning, there are almost 3 million people in New York City alone who live in neighbourhoods without reliable access to fresh foods.[2] Instead they are subject to packaged foods high in salt, sugar, and fat. These foods are one of the reasons our country has high rates of obesity and diabetes.[3] Furthermore, these packaged, processed foods create mounds upon mounds of waste in our landfills. Not only does food packaging create waste, so does the food itself. Seventeen percent of our landfills are made up of food scraps. Twenty million people could be fed each day if 25 percent of this thrown-away food was instead recovered.[4] Urban gardening is one way to build independence, provide fresh foods, and limit waste in the cities.

My friend Tasleema is a mother of three and an exemplary urban gardener. Her Brooklyn loft apartment is a totally unexpected urban oasis in the air. The loft is five hundred square metres, and on its roof deck are ripe fruits and vegetables growing everywhere, 'some', she says in a humble tone, 'growing out of reclaimed old dresser drawers and bookshelves.' Others grow in more traditional pots.'[5]

The bookshelves provide ready-made rows at a perfect depth for an urban rooftop garden. It is here that Tas grows kale, rainbow and green chard, strawberries, tomatoes, green beans, spinach, lettuce, ichiban eggplants, pumpkins, squash, cucumbers, and an assortment of herbs. 'New York City is a great place to be an urban farmer', she says. Tas feeds her family almost exclusively from her garden all through the summer months, and because of the relative warmth of the climate, she can pick things out of her garden well into November.

To water the plants in her rooftop garden, Tas has created a drip system made out of recycled bottles. For plants to grow, they need to drain: 'If the soil is too moist", she says, 'you'll kill the plant.' The water from the top plant therefore drains into the next, filters through its soil and drains into the next, and so on. It is like a domino watering system in which all the plants use the same water. Another step forward could be to employ a hydroponic system in which water could be circulated through the system and crops could be grown in smaller spaces.[6]

Many people erroneously think that cities don't have the space to plant and grow food, but urban rooftops are ideal places to have gardens. 'When I stand on my roof', Tas says, 'all I see are possible plots of land and farms, and food that could be.' She imagines the potential of the rooftop at her daughter's school and says, 'Young people could learn to grow the food they eat. It would teach responsibility.'

We talked about the need to get young people more involved in their diet, more conscious about the food choices they make, and about how they could end up holding their parents to higher standards. Planting and growing food themselves would take a lot of work — but this work could translate into a new appreciation of food and where it comes from.

Tas would like to see urban gardening grow to the point where people could plant things in the streets to feed the homeless. Her Deen orientates her toward what is good for her and for those around her — an expression of the principles of the Oneness of all creation (*tawhid*) and moving toward justice (*adl*). 'When you plant a seed', she says, 'you are patient, and the health benefits are much better than soda and a bag of crisps.' To that end, the goal of many serious urban 'foodies' like Tas is to get the food movement to the point that it is not just about buying and eating organic food, but about growing organic food in places where people cannot buy it.

Growing your own food is about striking a balance within the limits of your current and local reality. The basics that people have relied upon for centuries to propagate seedlings, water them, and transfer them to grow in the critical season are a part of being in balance with one's surroundings (*mizan*). Imagine rooftop and raised-bed gardens cropping up all over the city. One result would be cleaner air as plants pump oxygen into the exhaust-filled atmosphere. Some of the benefits are hidden, and Allah has dominion over the unseen. What we do know is that it is best to eat locally grown seasonal produce, and it is best to eat the food that comes from your own labour. This was the way of the Prophet Muhammad (peace be upon him), and this is the way of a Green Deen.

Is there a small strip of space lying unused, inside or out, that you can transform into the centrepiece of an urban or suburban garden?

Chapter 14

The Farmers' Market

While writing this book, I learned that food management is a clue to the priorities of a civilisation. The choices we make to transform our industrial food system into one that is localised will define our society as we move into the future.

Our current industrial system brings food to our tables from far away, and the financial and environmental costs of transportation are significant. Furthermore, the food is wrapped and packaged when it comes to our door, so once it's been consumed, there's still waste to get rid of. Moreover, the manufacture of this packaging is another process that supports the industrial system. Consumers with a Green Deen will want local fruits and vegetables that are pesticide-free and without wasteful plastic packaging.

Eating Healthily as Part of a Green Deen

Muslims are actively involved in bringing farm-fresh produce to local consumers. This chapter highlights Qaid Hassan, a Muslim who runs a farmers' market in Chicago, Illinois.[1]

Qaid grew up in Philadelphia, Pennsylvania, and, like me,

is a child of converts to Islam. He was raised in a Sister Clara
Muhammad School—named after the wife of Elijah Muhammad, longtime leader of the Nation of Islam, a group of African Americans who practiced a derivative form of Islam.[2]
Clara Muhammad schools are rigorous institutions of learning with a deep foundation in Islamic principles and are also
known for their healthy lunches.[3]

I learned a lot from Qaid when he came to visit me in
New York City, where I interviewed him at my house over
a healthy breakfast. We had gone to the store together and
had meticulously selected cage-free eggs, rice milk, locally
grown fruit, and Cabot cheese. Cabot is certified *halal* and
comes from free-range cows living on a cooperatively run
farm in Vermont. Cabot is a rarity—a mainstream brand in a
mainstream industry, but its production is anything but mainstream. I also had some maple butter I'd bought from a farmer
in the foothills of the Catskill Mountains, an area known for
environmentally friendly dairy farming.

We started our meal with oatmeal with apples, walnuts,
and a little maple butter, and as we went on to indulge in eggs
and dairy, I asked Qaid about his mostly vegetarian diet.
'Vegetarian eating', he said between bites, 'really allows us to
know more about the land and the food, about the different
varieties that are out there.' To Qaid, a diet heavy in meat goes
against the principle of living in balance with nature (*mizan*).
As he put it, 'Getting meat and poultry to our plates requires
so much energy that is not really returned to the Earth.' We
continued to discuss how Muslims, in general, probably need
to consume more fruits and vegetables.

Qaid's mother was raised Christian, but she raised her
children Muslim. She is also the proud owner of a successful

catering company. In her big family, she was always responsible for cooking the holiday feasts, and her love and skill in feeding hearty meals to large numbers of people resulted in her catering career. Qaid is proof that the apple doesn't fall too far from the tree.

As a young man, Qaid identified eating healthily as a foundational part of a Green Deen. So, being the energetic young college student he was, he thought to himself, 'Let me learn on an organic farm about how to grow food.' That farm was in Homestead, Florida, the southernmost town before the Everglades and the Florida Keys. 'It's an amazing, sunny, warm, jubilant place', he says. 'It had starfruit (carambola) and avocado trees, with a few raised beds of vegetables and herbs.' The main customers were large, upscale vendors from Miami. Here, swimming in the mangroves and sleeping under the stars, he began to recognise the *ayah*s (signs of Allah) found in nature. His food habits started to change. He began to harvest his own food and to compost the remains. All of this happened during a one-month winter break from college. He wasn't just farming; he was developing a whole new lifestyle that challenged him to really live as though he were aware of the covenant (*amanah*) between himself and God every day.

After graduating from Haverford College, a leading liberal arts school near Philadelphia, Qaid left to pursue graduate education at the University of Chicago. He was also in search of a new and thriving Muslim community, and soon thereafter he met his wife. He obtained a master's degree in business administration from the University of Chicago and set about finding ways to live his Deen integrated into the way he made a living. He wanted to make money in a way that would be aligned with the covenant, or trust (*amanah*) that humans have with God.

What ultimately drove Qaid's interest in wholesome food was being a new husband and preparing to be a father and trying to decide what he would do to feed his family the best possible food. Today, he runs a farmers' market in Chicago and has also recently started Whole Earth Meats, a purveyor of local, grass-fed, free-range, humanely raised meats and poultry that are both *dhabihah* and *halal*.[4] This is his family's source of food and income.[5]

Qaid's Inner-City Market

Operating a farmers' market in his new city seemed like a natural choice for Qaid, given that he was a practicing Muslim who was raised by a 'foodie' mother. 'It is simple and natural', he says, 'to try to preserve things in their natural course.' Healthy living and environmental stewardship (*khalifah*) is how Qaid manifests his Deen. Like most of us, Qaid had to discover his passion; carrying it out was a process that would take place over time.

Qaid's farmers' market, which brings local farmers into the city to sell their goods, is based in Chicago's Englewood community, an inner-city neighbourhood in which crime and poverty are rampant. It is precisely the kind of neighbourhood that would benefit greatly from locally grown fresh produce.

The idea of a marketplace is very familiar to Muslims. All around the Muslim world, the souk, as it is called, is the central gathering place of every town. The Prophet Muhammad (peace be upon him) has several hadith (sayings) that deal with the proper way to act and to transact business in the souk.[6]

Immigrant Muslims in the United States come with a deep spiritual connection to the marketplace.

For African Americans, bringing meat and produce from the farm to the urban community was once a common practice. In the 1950s and 1960s, African Americans maintained their connection to southern farms when they migrated to northern cities. These connections resulted in the import of food from southern farms to northern urban areas—farm-fresh foods that were otherwise not readily available there.[7] Tragically, those networks are long gone.

In some ways, what Qaid is doing with his farmers' market is reviving the traditions of those African American pioneers and mixing it with his Islamic sensibility. Islam orients Muslims toward living a life that is not wasteful, a life in which we are mindful of where our food comes from, and one in which we are careful not to create more harm, whether it is through our words, our actions, or our inaction. You, too, can be a part of this fusion of effort by finding local farmers, developing relationships with them, and using those relationships to feed your family with justice (the principle of *adl*)—justice to the farmer in paying a fair price and justice to the environment in minimising waste and maximising balance (*mizan*).

Farmers' markets are usually pricey for people used to buying low-quality foods from gas stations. Qaid's market, because of its location in the economically depressed neighbourhood of Englewood, has had a complicated financial struggle. Qaid wants to make sure that everything is affordable and accessible to this population, who desperately need it. To do so, he has had to find farmers willing to take a very low price for their goods—not less than what the products are worth, but less than the farmers could receive for them at other markets. Qaid has worked very hard in these negotiations and has been successful—as is evidenced by his market's robust activity.

In addition to bringing healthy food to Englewood, Qaid is committed to providing health education to the community's mainly African American and Latino residents. The market helps to increase their awareness about diabetes and hypertension, two chronic diseases that are prevalent but which can often be prevented through healthy eating.

What we learn from Qaid is that we can have strong internal values, value our relationship with the Creator, and make a living without compromising those values. It may seem as if Qaid is doing something completely new, but nothing is quite new—everything reasonates with something done before. Qaid is part of a time-honoured tradition in which urban dwellers, looking for healthy food for their families, establish relationships with farmers and make their living in the process.

Power to the People

As part of his commitment to living a Green Deen, Qaid believes in empowering other people through jobs. 'When you give people the opportunity to make their own money, in a way that benefits their surroundings, they're more likely to live an ethical and healthy life', he says.

Qaid wants to employ the people in the Englewood community as urban farmers. He wants them to create and work in urban gardens and to connect them to the process of getting their food from the root to the table. He wants to employ them as cooks and bakers and chefs and to give them the experience of canning, drying, and fermenting food. Qaid emphasises the importance and practicality of connecting with the planet, the principle of Oneness (*tawhid*). 'Getting your own food to your own table—you can't deny the practicality of that lifestyle', he says.

Qaid is not delusional. He understands that there are deep social problems in communities that prevent people from eating healthily. 'You can't have people lining up for green this and green that when a little girl's daily problem is that her mother's boyfriend is hitting her', he says. These challenges are very real for the social justice and environmental movements. In a society in which healthy eating has not been prioritised, other pervasive issues must be dealt with at the same time as trying to make healthy food a priority.

The Road Less Travelled

Muslims can be proactive about eating locally grown food and getting organic, grass-fed meat. Our communities are growing, we have resources, and we have the mosque as a centre. For Ramadan, we can get entire mosques to find local farmers and make just and healthy dealings that will bring seasonal, locally grown, healthy fruits and vegetables to our Iftar tables. For the Eid holiday, we can travel together to a farm and slaughter our own meat. We have the power to make these decisions.

I am reminded of the story of the Prophet Ibrahim (peace be upon him), when he was told by God to leave his wife and son and take his other son for sacrifice.[8] He was making choices that we cannot even imagine, choices that touch the essence of faith and understanding in Allah. It's with this faith that we can make decisions that seem hard to us—but which come with considerable benefits.

Following a Green Deen is taking the road less travelled. It's making tough choices and having faith in the Creator while making these choices. This spirit of takin the road less travelled is what the first generation of Muslims had when they were persecuted by the Quraysh, the tribe in Mecca from which the Prophet Muhammad (peace be upon him) came. It's the same energy that the companions of Jesus (may peace be upon him) held in their hearts—the spirit that compelled them to make the decision to walk a different path from everyone around them. It's the spirit my mother and father had when they left their childhood religion for Islam, and the spirit that Zachary Twist, Labinsky, and Ridwan Fallah, and Qaid Hassan all have as today they lead their families into following a Green Deen.

In the time of the Prophet (peace be upon him), the practices of life were based on using only whatever people had on hand. The emphasis was local and nonwasteful. In your time, what people do you know who are already applying these principles and creating simple and wholesome ways to feed their families and communities? Who are these folks with a Green Deen? How can you support them and become one of them?

Chapter 15

Green Dhabihah

Islam has a long-standing tradition of treating animals with respect and slaughtering meat in a clean and humane way. The best meat comes from animals who have enjoyed a *tayyib* (good) life. As part of following a Green Deen that affirms the Oneness (*tawhid*) of God and his creation, we need to look for humanely raised, grass-fed *halal* meat that is wrapped in environmentally friendly, non-wasteful packaging.

What We Have Is Something Beautiful

I have mentioned Yasir Syeed earlier in this book, for he is perhaps the most passionate and eloquent spokesperson for the role that the Deen, or the religion of Islam, plays in the larger movement for protecting the planet. 'It's not about organic, *halal,* grass fed', he says adamantly on the stage, flailing his arms and smiling. 'It is something much deeper.' Yasir wants to inspire you. 'We treat animals', he says, 'as though they are raw materials and humans are just consumers.'

Yasir sees a more noble role for humans, animals, all of creation. 'Everything in the heavens and the Earth does *dhikr* (remembrance of Allah)', he reminds us, quoting a scholar from another time when humans were better stewards (*khalifah*) of the Earth. 'All of creation has a spiritual essence, and a physical reality.'

Yasir is the founder, along with his wife, of an online service—GreenZabiha.com—that ships *halal,* grass-fed meat right to your doorstep. He does the slaughtering himself and is deeply in tune with the spiritual dimension that surrounds the practice of slaughtering as a sign (*ayah*) of God. The presence of animals in nature is a part of the balance (*mizan*) with which God has created the world. The Qur'an says:

> Do no mischief on the Earth after it has been set in order; but call on Him with fear and longing (in your hearts): for the mercy of Allah is (always) near to those who do good. (Qur'an 7:56)

And:

> Do they not look at the birds, held poised in the midst of (the air and) the sky? Nothing holds them up but (the power of) Allah. Surely in this are Signs for those who believe. (Qur'an 16:79)

I understand these *ayah*s (verses) to mean that no power exists besides that One Creator who perfectly ordered animals, plants, and humans to live here on this Earth. When we treat animals with disrespect, we destroy the divinely ordered balance of the universe.

Animal cruelty is forbidden in Islam. There are many examples from the time of the Prophet Muhammad (peace be upon him) that support this prohibition—for example: 'No human being kills a sparrow or [something] larger, without right, except that Allah will ask him about it on Judgment Day.' Someone asked the Holy Prophet (peace be upon him), 'What is the human's right over the animal?' The Holy Prophet (peace be upon him) replied, 'Its right is that you slaughter it and eat it, not that you decapitate it and throw it!'[1] This hadith allows an animal's death by human hands only for a very specific reason, such as for food.

Similarly, the Prophet Muhammad (peace be upon him) directed us to treat animals with love. They are not to be disrespected, denied food or water, or hurt in any way. The Holy Prophet (peace be upon him) once told the story of a woman who was punished because of a cat she had imprisoned until it died. 'She entered the (Hell) Fire because of it, for she neither gave the cat food nor water as she had imprisoned it, nor set it free to eat from the Earth.'[2] Killing and harming animals unjustly is unlawful and completely contradictory to the principles of balance (*mizan*) and justice (*adl*), which are part of a Green Deen.

There is clear direction in the Qur'an regarding what we can and cannot eat when it comes to meat:

He has only forbidden you dead meat, and blood, and the flesh of swine, and any (food) over which the name of other than Allah has been invoked. (Qur'an 16:115)

The Qur'an also states:

It is He Who has made the sea subject, that you may eat thereof flesh that is fresh and tender. (Qur'an 16:14)

This *ayah* makes seafood lawful to eat. The Qur'an goes further to prohibit eating animals that were strangled, beaten, or gorged. All of this is to make sure that even in ending an animal's life (for the purposes of food), it maintains its dignity.[3]

In Islam, there are three labels for meat—*halal, dhabihah,* and *tayyib.* *Halal* meat is lawful meat—any kind of poultry, beef, goat, and the like that has been slaughtered in a clean and humane way, even if it does not have the proper Islamic blessing of 'Bismillah Allahu Akbar' ('In the name of God, God is Great'). Traditionally, animals slaughtered by 'people of the book,' meaning Christians and Jews, are *halal* for Muslims to eat. *Dhabihah* meat is *halal* and also has been slaughtered with the proper blessing.

Tayyib meat comes from animals that were raised properly, fed properly, allowed to graze freely, and permitted to act in the most natural way—the way God intended.[4] In the early years of Islam, there was no factory farming industry. Therefore, animals were automatically raised properly. Today, when the meat industry is like any other—with profit margin as the bottom line—we have to be far more careful about how the animals that become our meat are raised and treated. They may not be meeting our Islamic guidelines.

Green Zabiha and the *Halal* Thanksgiving Turkey

Green Zabiha is an innovative company dedicated to providing *tayyib dhabihah* meat to Muslim and non-Muslim consumers. Founder Yasir Syeed agreed to take me on a visit to the Amish family farm he contracts with to get the company's organic grass-fed, free-range meat. His partnership with this farm is truly unique in that the owners allow him to slaughter the animals himself in the proper Islamic tradition.

I accompanied Yasir just before Thanksgiving to slaughter turkeys, and I immediately noticed how well the birds were living. They were walking around in a very large penned area, they were not crowded, and they were eating fresh grass. Yasir and I joked that their gobbling sounded like a chorus of 'Subhanallah!' ('Glorious is God').

Our goal was to catch and slaughter sixty turkeys, and I learned that day that catching turkeys is no easy task. Yasir and I ran around the grassy field until we were able to catch each turkey in a big bear hug. The turkeys were then put into a horse-drawn carriage and taken to be slaughtered.

Yasir had to teach me how to do the slaughtering in the Islamically appropriate way. First, one must sever the two jugular veins, the two carotid arteries, and the windpipe all together in one cut; at the very least, three of these need to be cut together. This ensures that all the blood is drained from the animal. Furthermore, the turkeys are prevented from seeing one another being slaughtered and also from seeing the knife blade being sharpened. The blade also cannot be serrated. Basically, according to Islamic tradition, the animal should suffer as little as possible.

With each of the turkeys we slaughtered that day, after the animal was dead and all the blood had been drained, we removed the head and then doused the body in warm water. We then removed the feathers and put our hands inside the body to pull the innards out. Once each turkey was cleaned, we vacuum-sealed it in plastic to be transported.

I was nervous holding the knife, so Yasir and I slaughtered the first turkey together. Before making the first cut, Yasir put his hand over mine, and in unison we recited the blessing 'Bismillah Allahuakbar', 'In the Name of God, God is Great.'

After one swift move, the blood gushed out warm over my cold fingers. I exhaled, washed my hands, put down the knife, and thought back to when I was eight years old and saw an animal being slaughtered for the first time.

It was during the Eid Al-Adha celebration that marks the end of the Hajj, the pilgrimage to Mecca that Muslims are required to make once in their lifetime. The Hajj is completed by sacrificing an animal to remember the Prophet Ibrahim (peace be upon him). Ibrahim was directed by Allah to sacrifice his son Ismail. Ibrahim's love of Allah and dedication to His command is what allowed him to take his son up to the top of a mountain, where God then replaced the child with a goat. This story was all about the mercy that God will show His followers should His command be respected.[5] As my father took me to watch the sacrificing of a lamb, he reminded me of this story of the prophet with whom I shared a name. I remembered how my father did everything according to the principles that I followed to sacrifice the turkey with Yasir. I also remember that the lamb, once sacrificed, looked as if it had simply fallen asleep.

My second thought after slaughtering that turkey was, How could one possibly kill a human being?

The Islamic slaughtering process is like a form of worship. 'It's like prayer', Yasir says. 'You don't want it reduced to a mechanical action. The same person should not be slaughtering each time. The idea is to understand the value of it. You are not supposed to let the process become rote.' Yasir was careful to wash his hands and to put his knife down between each slaughter. He is very conscious of how significant killing a living thing is. This animal just gave its life so that a human could eat. It is not a process to be taken lightly. You have to do the slaughter with presence. It is a physical, spiritual, and technical act. When the actual cut is being made, you recite 'Bismillah Allahu Akbar'—'In the Name of God, God is Great.' These words mean that you are doing it with Allah's permission.

We slaughtered all sixty turkeys that day, and each time I participated, I felt like I was in a state of prayer. The slaughtering did not become rote. I imagined all the Muslims who would be ordering those turkeys for their Thanksgiving feasts, and it made me calm to think about how each bird had lived a good life, roaming free in the pasture and eating grass. I thought about the disturbing ways in which factory-farmed animals are fed, raised, and slaughtered, and I thought to myself, I can always trust in Green Zabiha to provide healthy and happy meat.

I took one of the turkeys I slaughtered and presented it to my family as the official bird for our Thanksgiving. I will never forget that Thanksgiving. I made a prayer over the turkey before it went into the oven. When we cracked open the gizzard, it was filled with grass, a sign that it had been fed naturally. My aunt and mother collaborated on the preparation and cooking, and the bird was roasted to perfection. Most of my family members are not Muslim, and this Thanksgiving turkey was an opportunity to share something about my faith that I felt strongly about—that animals should be treated humanely and be slaughtered in the best way possible. At the same time, the turkey provided a powerful lesson on taste—a grass-fed turkey just tastes better!

There is an alternative to factory-farmed meat. The framework is simple: free-range, grass-fed, and blessed. Build a partnership with a local farmer who is committed to organic farming. The animals will be nitrate-free, antibiotic-free, and without growth hormones. They will be healthy, and healthy for you to eat. Look for food that is double-certified as both organic and *halal*—it comes from companies that have their eye on more than just their profit margin.

I will leave you with a question Yasir posed one day in our many talks as I prepared this book:

'What do you feed cat food to?' he asked.

'A cat', I replied.

'What do you feed dog food to?' he asked,

'A dog', I replied in kind.

Finally, he asked, 'What do you feed junk food to?'

He answered his own question: 'To people who think they are junk.'

Think about your community. What can be done to ensure that the food your family eats meets the highest of standards? How can you work together with your fellow brothers and sisters of all faiths to ensure that eating healthily and spirituality are on the same page?

Chapter 16

American Halal—Setting the Stage for the Future

In an industry that runs on marketing information, Adnan Durrani has become a master of managing data and trends that will inform tough decisions. He is a compelling figure in the growing *halal* food marketplace because he has had proven success running a large business in the past. He is uniquely positioned to making *halal* and organically grown, ethically raised meat and vegetables a staple of the American and Canadian diet—Muslim or not. Adnan is also a connector of like-minded Muslims all over the world and an interfaith leader who regularly engages in dialogue with people from all walks of life. With his knowledge base, network, and vision, he is setting the table for the future of *halal* and organic eating.

Adnan is an ethical entrepreneur and a responsible and ethical investor who starts and supports firms that reflect his values. We first met in 2006 at a conference of entrepreneurs seeking to develop a 'caring capitalism'.[1] In one of the ses-

sions on the environmental movement, I made the observation that the 'green movement' needs to be better connected
to communities of faith, which already have a vested interest
in protecting the planet. Afterward, Adnan identified himself
as Muslim and asked if I knew where the mosque in Tucson
was. I did know, and he and I drove over for Friday congrega-
tional prayer. Over the years we have stayed in touch, partly
because he understands his role as a steward (*khalifah*) of the
Earth and wants to leave it better than he found it. Adnan also
recognises the importance of developing talent to help build
an industry and has begun mentoring young entrepreneurs
with good ideas and a strong commitment to a Green Deen.

Stonyfield Farms

One of the most successful companies Adnan was involved
with was the yogurt brand Stonyfield Farms. Early on,
Stonyfield came across the same concerns facing a lot of small
companies that are trying to do something new while staying
true to their values. Its founders were committed to providing organic yogurt from cows that lived on farms free from
toxic pesticides, and so resigned themselves to paying double
the manufacturing costs with very low margins. 'That's a very
tough business model to make a profit with', Adnan said, 'so
we had to find a different way to make a profit.'

Stonyfield found a way to stress its principles and value
system and its mission around food and planet, just as Qaid,
Yasir, and scores of others have done. Stonyfield learned that
values are something consumers will pay attention to and
when given the clear choice, they will choose the product that
is most aligned with their moral principles.

American Halal Company, Inc.

Today, Adnan is the chief operating officer (COO) of American Halal Company, Inc., but he calls himself the CHO, or chief *halal* officer. He is also a networker and a connector extraordinaire who has worked with rising stars in the *halal* world, such as Shahed Amanullah of Zabiha.com, which provides an online searchable database of *halal* restaurants and locations all over the country. A skilled executive, Adnan now has a deep understanding of the *halal* market, its potential, and the demographics of the Muslim American population. He knows there is considerable opportunity in following the principles of a Green Deen, which recognise that everything in the universe is connected (*tawhid*) and that our actions reflect our values. Adnan is not afraid to share what he knows with other ambitious and values-oriented businesspeople.

At the 2009 American Muslim Consumer Conference, Adnan asked the audience: 'What are the trends in the food market?' He answered his own question with: 'We're seeing back-to-the-future, simple appeals—especially after the financial crisis—going back to the less-is-more.'[2]

Less is more. Adnan was describing everything I've discussed in part IV of this book—sustainable and local farming, treating animals humanely, eating seasonally, and following Green Deen principles to feed your family. He was also speaking to the right crowd, as they were as diverse as the U.S. Muslim community, many of whom come from countries, societies, and cultural traditions whose impact on the environment is considerably less than that of the average American. Because this particular audience already recognised that people's behaviour and attitudes must alter and that consumption patterns need to shift, Adnan sounded a hopeful note while keeping history and trends in mind, saying, 'The stage is set for a *halal* premium brand—just look at the kosher industry. Today it's a $10 billion market and still growing at 15 percent a year.' Even in this economic crisis, consumers are willing to pay for socially responsible products.

A whole generation of Muslims is living a Green Deen. They respect and value nature and want to see the signs (*ayat*) of God protected so they can enjoy and benefit from them; they seek out opportunities to move toward justice (*adl*) by serving their community; and they respect the fact that disturbing the balance (*mizan*) causes injustice.

Consumer Power

You can see 'American *halal*' manifest itself in the choices consumers are willing to make, demanding from companies higher-quality food—quality with the triple bottom line of profit, benefit to people, and benefit to the Earth. Consumers want to have food that is antibiotic-free, ethically packaged, free-range, fair-trade, tasty, and *halal*. Opportunity exists, it seems, for the edgy and savvy producer of a product with all the right mix of social-justice, eco-friendly, and high-quality characteristics—a producer that markets to a powerful audience: Muslim consumers.

My wife and I are examples of this powerful market. We are young, Muslim, educated, concerned about the environment, and willing to invest in socially responsible companies. We are trying to live a Green Deen and are looking for companies that will help us. At a talk I delivered at the ADAMS Center in Virginia,[3] I was told by a man at the end of the talk that he and his family had decided there was more value for them to buy meat that was not *halal,* but meat that was raised the right way. Therefore, they would travel a little further and pay a bit more to go to a luxury grocery store that specialised in organic meats.

There are many more like us out there grappling with this decision, and new options are now cropping up all over the country. Recently Qaid Hassan started his Whole Earth Meats, which operates in the Chicago area (see chapter 14); Norwich Meadow Farm in upstate New York provides organic produce and *halal* meats; and projects are underway to link these and other such efforts. The network that Adnan Durrani, Yasir Syeed of GreenZabiha.com (see chapter 15), and Qaid Hassan are part of will grow exponentially in the next five to ten years, thanks to the growing demand for food production with Green Deen principles.

Take a step back from the food you eat and think about where it comes from. Once in a while, as the Qur'an tells us, we should actually reflect on the world around us, and connect a little bit more to the natural world. Wouldn't we feel that sense of awe? Don't you want to feel there is a blessing in each and every bite?

Following the Call

Al-salamu alaykum, Peace and Blessings be unto you.

You have just been taken through a collection of thoughts, stories, and practical pieces of advice to help you further your Green Deen. You have read *ayah*s and hadith that provide some insight into Islam's position on the environment. You have seen moments of success—such as the creation of innovative and 'back-to-the-future' companies like Whole Earth Meats and Green Zabiha. And you have seen moments of pause that compel you to reflect—such as the environmental and human harm caused by mountaintop coal removal and the ongoing BP oil disaster in the Gulf of Mexico. I hope that throughout this book you have been inspired to join the movement to protect the planet and are curious to learn more.

In some ways, this book is a response to what I see as an oversecularised environmental movement. As a person of faith who works to protect the planet because of his faith, I feel that too many like me are being left out of the global environmental discussion. The original Green Muslim in the United States, Seyyed Hossein Nasr, author of *Man and Nature: The Spiritual Crisis in Modern Man,* makes the following observation:

> As awareness of the environmental crisis has increased, numerous vocal groups and even political parties have sprung up to defend the environment. Until recently, however, most of these have had a leftish tendency with a tone decisively opposed to established religions, although this is now changing, somewhat, . . . while some have sought to convert the ecological movement into a religion itself.[1]

There is a lot of 'greenwashing' out in the world today. I applaud those who consider themselves 'green' because of their submission to marketing ploys—doing something is always better than doing nothing. However, I do question the level of commitment that some people truly have to the environment. The corporate 'profits over people' mantra has infiltrated the environmental movement, as have fear-based messages, false hopes, and an obsession with data. Transforming the world, its people, and their behaviour will not be motivated by fear tactics and empty hope and statistics. The amount of carbon per person that is emitted into the atmosphere will not make any hearts leap. Overwhelming 'evidence' and a decision from environmental 'elites' will not make the change. What will inspire change is connecting the planet to each person's self-interest and ensuring each person's understanding of the issues.

We desperately need to 'meet people where they're at.' We cannot expect the vast majority of the population to magically know everything that an expert would—a common mistake made by the movement. Assumptions are made about citizens, governments, corporations, and even the natural resources that don't have a voice of their own.

I learned that to meet people where they're at, you must first leave your comfort zone. This lesson came to me in 2008 when I was in Memphis, Tennessee, for the Dream Reborn conference, organised by Green For All. It was a gathering of black and brown 'greenies' and their allies who celebrated the life of Dr. Martin Luther King Jr. and presented positive solutions for social and environmental equity. I was surrounded by an insular community of environmentalists, loudly 'preaching to the choir'. Who was listening? I was desperate to find out.

I wandered off the convention grounds into downtown Memphis and found a small restaurant, where a local woman asked what brought me from New York. In typical northeastern/liberal/elitist fashion, I answered her question with a question: 'What do you think about global warming?' I really wanted to know what the local people thought. She didn't hesitate in her response.

'You know', she said, 'it sounds like the Democrats are trying to get me to be afraid of something.'

I was stunned. "What do you mean by that?" I asked.

Again she didn't hesitate: 'You know, the same way the Republicans are always trying to get me to be afraid of terrorism.'

Fear is one way to motivate people, but it leads to despair. So is hope, but it can lead to inaction. The real trick is to find the right common language to connect with people, but also to put stock in the importance of people's understanding.

I understand that the United States of America was founded on principles of promoting the general welfare of its citizens. In the Declaration of Independence, the pursuit of happiness and freedom is often associated with economic freedom. Freedom and economics were seen as essential to each other. Today, 'freedom' often means the freedom to buy and to consume. No longer is there an innate exceptionality to each citizen and human in the land. We are now only relevant to the state insomuch as we can work, spend, shop, consume, and use. Materialism and overconsumption have resulted in a reduction of the human experience to units of production and consumption. A Green Deen is rooted in the exceptionality of individuals who will one day be held accountable to their Creator. How we manage waste, watts, water, and food—and, most important, ourselves—is beyond a marketing ploy: it is a Deen, a path, a way, a calling.

Our Green Deen says we need to look critically at economic injustice and to address the roots (not the fruits) of the environmental problem. The core of a new vision that can effectively form a more perfect union is multisector and multifaith. This vision includes a new slate of policy reforms, some of which have already begun. This is a new era of executive leadership and accountability, a new era of legislative focus. It is a time of community organising, interfaith activism, and innovation across sectors.

How we manage waste, watts, water, and food should reinforce the moral foundations of our communities. It should also ensure economic and social justice and move away from entitlement toward empowerment. By strengthening the work of previous generations, we can offer a new economic freedom: the freedom to transform our pollution-based 'grey' economy to one that affirms life, one that is sustainable and 'green'. Through this process, we connect with the planet and affirm the Oneness of all in creation, the interconnectivity of life. We recognise that the signs of the Creator are all around us, and we move toward justice as we maintain the balance that Allah created. We hold in high regard our trust from God to be His representatives on the Earth.

We praise our Creator, take care of our planet, and take care of each other.

Ameen.

Notes

Preface

1. For most of the translations of the *ayah*s quoted in this book, I have relied upon Yusuf Ali's *The Meanings of the Illustrious Qur'an* (Brooklyn, NY: Al Arqam Dawa Center, 2006), www.alarqamdawa center.com.

Introduction: The Earth Is a Mosque

1. *Masjid* means mosque in Arabic, and an imam is a religious leader of a mosque. Imam Siraj is one of the leaders of the U.S. Muslim community.

2. *Sahih Muslim,* trans. Abdul Hamid Siddiqi (Beirut: Dar Al Arabia, n.d.), book 4: hadith 1057.

3. Abdul Mannan Omar, *Dictionary of the Holy Qur'an,* 3rd ed. (Delaware: Noor Foundation, 2005), 185.

4. Pew Forum on Religion and Public Life, *Mapping the Global Muslim Population: A Report on the Size and Distribution of the World's Muslim Population* (Washington, DC: 2009).

5. Remarks made by Yasir Sayeed at the Islamic Society of North America National Convention, Rosemont, IL, 3 July 2010.

6. Afzalur Rahman, vol. 1, *Liberty, Readings in Political Philosophy* (London: Seerah Foundation, 1987), 13.

7. Qur'an 25:53 and 55:19–20.

8. Qur'an 23:12–14.

9. Lamont C. Hempel, *Environmental Governance: The Global Challenge* (Washington DC: Island Press, 1996), 91.

10. Faraz Khan, lectures on Islam and the Environment, Columbia University, New York, 19 February 2010.

11. Richard C. Foltz, Frederick M. Denny, and Azizan Baharuddin, eds., *Islam and Ecology: A Bestowed Trust* (Cambridge, MA: Harvard University Press, 2003), 253–54.

12. *Sahih Muslim,* book 10: hadith 10 (see n. 2).

13. John M. Balbus, 'Identifying Vulnerable Subpopulations for Climate Change Health Effects', *Journal of Occupational and Environmental Medicine* 51 (2009): 33–37.

14. Imam Zaid Shakir, personal communication.

15. Islamic Society of North America Annual Conference, Chicago, IL, 4 July 2010.

16. *Sahih Muslim,* book 10: hadith 10 (see n. 2).

PART I Waste

Chapter 1: The Problem of Overconsumption

1. *Sahih Muslim,* trans. Abdul Hamid Siddiqi (Beirut: Dar Al Arabia, n.d.), book 10: hadith 10.

2. *Sahih Al-Bukhari,* trans. Muhammad Muhsin Khan (Ankara: Islamic University, Al Medina Al Munauwara, n.d.), book 10: hadith 10.

3. For these concepts I am indebted to Annie Leonard's *The Story of Stuff: How Our Obsession with Stuff Is Trashing the Planet, Our Communities, and Our Health—and a Vision for Change* (New York, Free Press, 2010), www.storyofstuff.com, and to Seyyed Hossein

Nasr's *Man and Nature: The Spiritual Crisis in Modern Man* (Chicago: ABC International, 1997).

4. Lamont C. Hempel, *Environmental Governance: The Global Challenge* (Washington DC: Island Press, 1996), 54.

Chapter 2: The Environmental Movement as a Response to Overconsumption

1. Albert Memmi, *The Colonizer and the Colonized* (Boston: Beacon Press, 1967).

2. Muhammad Baqir al-Sadr, *Islam and Schools of Economics* (Pakistan: Islamic Seminary Publications, 1979), 16.

3. Ibid., 18–20.

4. Ibid., 16–18.

5. Barack Obama, 'Remarks by the President on a New Beginning, Cairo University, Cairo, Egypt,' press release, 4 June, 2009, http://www.whitehouse.gov/the-press-office/remarks-president-cairo-university-6-04-09.

6. U.S. Department of State, 'Background Note: Indonesia', www.state.gov/r/pa/ei/bgn/2748.htm.

7. Sunanda Creagh, 'Time Needed for Indonesia Environment Law: Official', Reuters, 16 October, 2009, www.reuters.com/article/idUSTRE59F0T220091016.

8. See http://www.sustainablebusiness.com/index.cfm/go/news.display/id/20585for examples.

9. 'Green Building Council Indonesia Issues Green Building Rating Tools', *Jakarta Post,* http://www.thejakartapost.com/news/2010/06/17/green-building-council-indonesia-issues-green-building-rating-tools.html.

10. Library of Congress, 'The Evolution of the Conservation Movement, 1850–1920', http://memory.loc.gov/ammem/amrvhtml/conshome.html.

11. Theodore Roosevelt, 'New Nationalism' speech, given in

Osawatomie, Kansas, on 31 August, 1910, http://teachingamerican
history.org/library/index.asp?document=501.

12. New York City Department of Parks and Recreation, 'Fort
Greene Park', www.nycgovparks.org/parks/FortGreenePark.

13. Library of Congress, 'Evolution of the Conservation
Movement' (see n. 10).

14. Lamont C. Hempel, *Environmental Governance: The Global
Challenge* (Washington DC: Island Press, 1996), 119.

15. U.S. Environmental Protection Agency, 'Clean Air Act:
Title II: Emissions Standards for Moving Sources', www.epa.gov/
air/caa/title2.html.

16. Seyyed Hossein Nasr, *Man and Nature: The Spiritual Crisis
in Modern Man* (Chicago: ABC International, 1997). Originally
published as *Man and Nature: The Spritual Crisis of Modern Man*
(London: Unwin, 1976).

17. U.S. Environmental Protection Agency, 'Summary of the
Resource Conservation and Recovery Act', www.epa.gov/lawsregs/
laws/rcra.html.

18. Charles Brown, Christopher Norwood, Melissa Brown, and
Elizabeth Green, presentation on 'Exploring our World Through
Building Environmental and Social Justice', New York, 29 January,
2009.

19. Michael Shellenberger and Ted Nordhaus, 'The Death
of Environmentalism: Global-Warming Politics in a Post-
Environmental World' (2004), www.thebreakthrough.org/PDF/
Death_of_Environmentalism.pdf.

20. Ibid.

21. Manami Kano and Vivian Chang, 'Enviro-Justice Activists
Send a Dispatch from a Panel with the Reapers', 4 March, 2005,
http://grist.org/politics/chang-2/.

22. Van Jones, *The Green Collar Economy: How One Solution Can
Fix Our Two Biggest Problems* (New York: HarperCollins, 2008).

23. *Shamaa-il Timidhi,* trans. Muhammad Bin Abdur Rahman Ebrahim (New Delhi: Adam Publishers), hadith 13.

Chapter 3: Green Muslims

1. *Shamaa-il Timidhi,* trans. Muhammad Bin Abdur Rahman Ebrahim (New Delhi: Adam Publishers), hadith 8.

2. The material in this section is from an interview with Aziz Siddiqi by the author.

3. The information in this section was gathered over the course of several conversations between Sarah Sayeed and the author in the summer and fall of 2009.

4. Comments made at 22 April, 2010, Faith Leaders for Environmental Justice Breakfast.

5. Ninth Annual Interfaith Iftar Fast Break, 'Diet or Buy It? Faith, Food, and Resource Consumption', co-hosted by the Union Theological Seminary, the Muslim Consultative Network, and the Interfaith Center of New York, in partnership with the Columbia University Muslim Students Association, held at the Union Theological Seminary, 15 September, 2009. The panelists were Liore Milgrom-Elcott, associate director of special projects at Hazon; Imam Muhammad Hatim, Admiral Family Circle Islamic Community and Visiting Professor GTS; Naresh Jain, National and International Jain representative; Dr. Hal Taussig, Visiting Professor of New Testament, Union Theological Seminary; and moderator, Ibrahim Abdul-Matin.

6. Ibid.

7. The material in this section is from number of conversations between Sarah Jawaid and the author in October of 2009.

8. All Dulles Area Muslim Society, *Green Environment Guide* (Washington, DC: Adams Center, 2009), AdamsCenter.org.

9. Quotations from Sarah Jawaid and the following informa-

tion on the DC Green Muslims are from an interview with Sarah Jawaid by the author.

Chapter 4: Green Mosques

1. City of New York, *PlaNYC: A Greener, Greater New York* (New York: Mayor's Office of Long Term Planning and Sustainability, 2009). See http://www.nyc.gov/html/planyc2030/html/home/home.shtml.

2. 'Mayor Bloomberg and Speaker Quinn Announce Major Package of Legislation to Create Greener, Greater Buildings Plan for New York City', press release, 9 December, 2009.

3. Lamont C. Hempel, *Environmental Governance: The Global Challenge* (Washington DC: Island Press, 1996), 92.

4. Naser I. Faruqui, 'Islam and Water Management: Overview and Principles', International Development Research Centre, http://idrc.org/es/ev-93948-201-1-DO_TOPIC.html.

5. Faruqui, 'Islam and Water Management'.

6. Peter C. Frumhoff et al., *Confronting Climate Change in the U.S. Northeast: Science, Impacts, Solutions,* Synthesis Report of the Northeast Climate Impacts Assessment (Cambridge, MA: Union of Concerned Scientists, 2007), www.climatechoices.org/assets/documents/climatechoices/confronting-climate-change-in-the-u-s-northeast.pdf.

7. Author's trip to Hawaii, 2007.

8. The description of this small mosque is from an interview with Fatima Ashraf by the author.

9. Author's trip to Tucson, Arizona, 2006.

10. Mairi Beautyman, 'Students Plan Green Future for Mosques in Abu Dhabi', *Huffington Post,* 10 June, 2009, www.huffingtonpost.com/mairi-beautyman/students-plan-green-futur_b_213972.html.

11. Islamic Foundation for Ecology and Environmental Sci-

ences, 'Is Your Mosque an Eco Mosque: Singapore', http://ifees.org .uk/index.php?option=com_content&task=view&id=58&Itemid=56.

12. Laura Thistlethwaite, 'Muslims Put Faith in £3.5m Eco-Mosque', *South Manchester Reporter,* 3 July, 2008, www.south manchesterreporter.co.uk/news/s/1056667_muslims_put_faith_in _35m_ecomosque.

13. We can get help to do this from our interfaith friends at GreenFaith, who have started outlining ways that congregations can do the education 'greening' alongside some simple steps the faith house can do going forward. See GreenFaith: Interfaith Partners in Action for the Earth, 'Getting Started in Your House of Worship—Six Ideas for Getting Started', www.greenfaith.org/ files/getting-started-6-steps.

14. Pew Forum on Religion and Public Life, *Mapping the Global Muslim Population: A Report on the Size and Distribution of the World's Muslim Population* (Washington, DC: 2009), 1.

15. The following material on the Ash-Shaheed Islamic Center is from a series of interviews with Aidah Muhammad by the author in November 2009.

16. Ibrahim Abdul-Matin, data gathered as part of an unpublished study commissioned by the Inner-City Muslim Action Network, 2009.

17. The People's Grocery (not part of the Lighthouse Mosque) addresses disparities of health and wealth in West Oakland with their emphasis on helping people learn the how and the why of accessing and preparing whole foods. See www.peoplesgrocery.org/ article.php/westoakland.

18. I was blessed to have Imam Zaid Shakir edit a copy of *Green Deen* in its early stage. The copy was very different from the document you now hold, and that is due in large part to his reorientating my approach through his finely tuned red ink. Please include him and his efforts in your *dua*s (supplications). Imam Zaid is a true Green Imam!

19. All Dulles Area Muslim Society, *Adams Green Environment Guide* (Washington, DC: Adams Center, 2009), AdamsCenter.org.

20. *Sahih Muslim,* trans. Abdul Hamid Siddiqi (Beirut: Dar Al Arabia, n.d.), book 10: hadith 10.

PART II: Watts

Chapter 5: Energy from Hell

1. Albert Hourani, *A History of the Arab Peoples* (New York: Warner Books, 1991), 320; John W. Limbert, *Negotiating with Iran: Wrestling the Ghosts of History* (Washington DC: United States Institute of Peace Press, 2009), 67. Pages 59–87 give considerable background information on the political crisis, personalities, and intrigue that pervaded in the period of the oil nationalisation crisis of 1951–1953.

2. Interestingly, the Islamic Republic of Iran included an ideological commitment to environmental protection in its 1979 constitution. Article 50 reads: 'In the Islamic Republic protection of the natural environment, in which present and future generations must lead an ever-improving community life, is a public obligation. Therefore all activities, economic or otherwise, which may cause irreversible damage to the environment are forbidden.' Richard C. Foltz, Frederick M. Denny, and Azizan Baharuddin, eds., *Islam and Ecology: A Bestowed Trust* (Cambridge, MA: Center of World Religions, Harvard Divinity School, 2003), 259, 261.

3. REDOIL, 'Oil and the Alaska Native Claims Settlement Act', www.ienearth.org.

4. The following material on the Alaska National Wildlife Refuge is from an interview with Faith Gemmill by the author on 15 September, 2009.

5. National Oceanic and Atmospheric Administration (NOAA), 'Federal Science Report Details Fate of Oil from BP Spill', 4 August, 2010, www.noaanews.noaa.gov/stories2010/20100804_oil.html.

6. Fiona Harvey and Thomas Dinham, 'Experts Split over Level of BP Oil Spill Damage', *Financial Times* (London), 9 August, 2010, www.ft.com/cms/s/0/b4154478-a3ea-11df-9e3a-00144feabdc0 .html?ftcamp=rss.

7. Arjun Makhijani, *Carbon-Free and Nuclear-Free: A Roadmap for U.S. Energy Policy* (Maryland: IEER Press, 2007), 79.

8. Massoud Amin and Bruce F. Wollenberg, 'Toward a Smart Grid', *IEEE Power and Energy Magazine* 3 (2005): 34–38.

9. 'Learn More About Mountaintop Removal Coal Mining: Frequently Asked Questions', iLoveMountains.org, www.ilove mountains.org/resources; Sierra Club, 'Interior Department Stuck in Slow Motion on Addressing Mountaintop Removal Coal Mining', press release, 19 November, 2009, http://action.sierraclub. org/site/MessageViewer?em_id=145001.0.

10. Tim Thornton, 'A Death in Inman', *Roanoke Times,* 3 July, 2006, www.roanoke.com/news/nrv/mountaintop/wb/71870; Tim Thornton, 'Southwest Virginia Family and A&G Coal Settle in 3-Year-Old's Death', *Roanoke Times,* 24 July, 2010, www.roanoke .com/news/nrv/wb/81731.

11. Kari Lydersen, 'West Virginia Town Fights Blanket of Coal Dust', *New Standard*, 9 May, 2006, http://www.minesandcommu-nities.org/article.php?a=5711; interview with anti-coal organizer Stephanie Tyree by the author, October 2009.

12. Interview with anti-coal organiser Stephanie Tyree by the author, October 2009

13. Sierra Club, 'Interior Department Stuck in Slow Motion on Addressing Mountaintop Removal Coal Mining', press release, 19 November, 2009, http://action.sierraclub.org/site/Message Viewer?em_id=145001.0.

14. Ibid.

15. Interview with anti-coal organiser Stephanie Tyree by the author, October 2009.

16. "Some Interesting Oil Industry Statistics—Most Frequently

Asked Questions: Oil in the Gulf of Mexico', Gibson Consulting
Online, www.gravmag.com/faq.shtml.

Chapter 6: Energy from Heaven

1. I was attending that rally for green in Washington, DC,
because I was one of the key national organisers of the Green Jobs
Now! movement. I got the 'energy from heaven' framework from
comments made that day.

2. As noted in the preface to this book, for most of the Qur'anic
translations of meaning, I have relied upon Abdullah Yusuf Ali's
The Meanings of the Illustrious Qur'an (Brooklyn, NY: Al Arqam
Dawa Center, 2006), www.alarqamdawacenter.com.

3. Arjun Makhijani, Carbon-Free and Nuclear-Free: A Roadmap for U.S. Energy Policy (Maryland: IEER Press, 2007), 60.

4. Information on Yusef Miller and Barbara Grant and the
work of Photovoltaics Plus is from an interview with Rasul Miller
by the author on 31 October, 2009.

5. Ibid.

6. The first words spoken by Winona LaDuke as she took the
podium as a vice-presidential candidate appearing with presidential candidate Ralph Nader at the Fleet Center in Boston, MA, in
2000, an event attended by the author.

7. "Alternative Energy/Wind Power (Gaa-Noodin-oke),' White
Earth Land Recovery Project and Native Harvest Online Catalog,
http://nativeharvest.com/. As stated in the article: 'Our reservation's western region has a class four wind potential. As well, we sit
on the cusp of the Great Plains, considered to be the Saudi Arabia
of Wind Power by most energy analysts.'

8. It was a real blessing to meet Winona LaDuke at the
Good Jobs Green Jobs Conference on 4–6 February, 2009, in
Washington, DC. Here also is where I first asked Congressman
Keith Ellison to write the foreword for *Green Deen*.

9. 'Energy Development for Indians: Harvesting the Air—Tribes Struggle to Develop New Projects on the Plains', *Economist*, 31 March, 2010.

10. Massoud Amin and Bruce F. Wollenberg, 'Toward a Smart Grid', *IEEE Power and Energy Magazine* 3 (2005): 34–38.

11. Interview with Haider Akmal by the author, 20 November, 2009.

12. Makhijani, *Carbon-Free and Nuclear-Free*, 144.

Chapter 7: Efficiency and Green Jobs

1. At this time, I was working closely with Green For All (www.greenforall.org), whose mission is 'Working to build an inclusive green economy strong enough to lift people out of poverty.' I ended up being a member of their Green For All Academy (see www.greenforall.org/what-we-do/building-a-movement/fellows-class-1).

2. Comments delivered at the first Green For All retreat at the Garrison Institute, 10–13 January, 2008, Garrison, NY.

3. Van Jones, *The Green Collar Economy: How One Solution Can Fix Our Two Biggest Problems* (New York: Harper Collins, 2008).

4. *Sahih Al-Bukhari,* trans. Muhammad Muhsin Khan (Ankara: Islamic University, Al Medina Al Munauwara, n.d.), book 71: hadith 618.

5. Jay Inslee and Bracken Hendricks, *Apollo's Fire: Igniting America's Clean Energy Economy* (Washington DC: Island Press, 2008), 100. Bracken Hendricks should also get some credit for helping me to seed the idea for this book. He and I shared breakfast with Laurie and Kalia Leyshon (founders of the Massachusetts Green Jobs Coalition) at an energy conference in western Massachusetts in early 2009, where he lamented that there was no Muslim voice involved in the green economy movement.

6. *A National Green Building Research Agenda* (U.S. Green

Building Council Research Committee report, November 2007, www.usgbc.org/ShowFile.aspx?DocumentID=3402.

7. Van Jones quotation taken from the author's notes at the White House green jobs summit.

8. Middle Class Task Force, Council on Environmental Quality, *Recovery Through Retrofit,* October 2009, http://www.whitehouse.gov/assets/documents/Recovery_Through_Retrofit_Final_Report.pdf.

Chapter 8: Living off the Grid

1. Initially Kathy did not plan on taking a Muslim name until she came upon the story of Umaya and took the name because it reasonated with her.

2. Dennis Scanlin, 'The Design, Construction and Use of an Indirect, Through-Pass, Solar Food Dryer', *Home Power Magazine* 57 (1997): 62–72.

PART III Water

1. Akan and Yoruba are two traditional African religions that honour the spirits in water in its different manifestations.

2. *Sahih Al-Bukhari,* trans. Muhammad Muhsin Khan (Ankara: Islamic University, Al Medina Al Munauwara, n.d.), book 10: hadith 10.

Chapter 9: Water: Essential for Survival

1. Alan Ward, 'Weighing Earth's Water from Space', NASA Earth Observatory, http://earthobservatory.nasa.gov/Features/WeighingWater.

2. South African Faith Communities' Environment Institute, 'Jumu'ah Khutbah on the Conservation of Water by the Muslim Judicial Council', http://safcei.org/oldsite/oldsite/news/view.php%3Fid=8.html.

3. 'Water Facts', Water.org, http://water.org/learn-about-the
-water-crisis/facts.

4. Ibid.

5. "Water, Our Thirsty World," *National Geographic,* April
2010, 55.

6. *Sahih Al-Bukhari,* trans. Muhammad Muhsin Khan (Ankara:
Islamic University, Al Medina Al Munauwara, n.d.), book 10:
hadith 10.

7. Ibid., book 40, hadith 547.

8. Jonathan D. Miller, *Infrastructure 2010: An Investment
Imperative* (Washington, DC: Urban Land Institute, 2010).

9. *Sahih Al-Bukhari,* book 10, hadith 10.

10. 'Water, Our Thirsty World', *National Geographic,* April
2010, 32.

Chapter 10: Toxic Waste in Our Water

1. Robert Emmet Hernan, *This Borrowed Earth: Lessons from the
Fifteen Worst Environmental Disasters Around the World* (New York:
Palgrave Macmillan, 2010), 9–13.

2. 'Interior Department Stuck in Slow Motion on Addressing
Mountaintop Removal Coal Mining', Sierra Club press
release, 19 November, 2009, http://action.sierraclub.org/site/
MessageViewer?em_id=145001.0.

3. The following material on mountaintop removal coal mining
comes from an interview with anti-coal activist Stephanie Tyree by
the author in October 2009. Stephanie is a tireless water-quality
and anti–mountaintop coal removal advocate. She fights for people
in her home state, frames her work around environmental justice,
and gave me reams of valuable insight as a background for this
entire issue.

4. Most of the material in the groundwater contamination section comes from an interview with Tauhirah Abdul-Matin by the
author on 7 March, 2010.

5. For a list of the compounds that fall under each contaminant group, see www.epa.gov/safewater/contaminants/index.html.

6. 'Coca-Cola's "Toxic" India Fertiliser: Waste Product from a Coca-Cola Plant in India Which the Company Provides as Fertiliser for Local Farmers Contains Toxic Chemicals, a BBC Study Has Found,' *BBC News,* 25 July, 2003, http://news.bbc.co.uk/2/hi/south_asia/3096893.stm.

7. India Resource Center, Campaign to Hold Coca-Cola Responsible, 'Coca-Cola Crisis in India,' www.indiaresource.org/campaigns/coke.

8. Maude Barlow and Tony Clarke, *Blue Gold: The Fight to Stop the Corporate Theft of the World's Water* (New York: New Press, 2002), 22.

9. 'Aquafina Labels to Spell Out Source—Tap Water', Reuters, 27 July, 2007, http://edition.cnn.com/2007/HEALTH/07/27/pepsico.aquafina.reut/.

10. Natural Resources Defense Council, 'Bottled Water: Pure Drink or Pure Hype?' http://www.nrdc.org/water/drinking/bw/bwinx.asp.

11. Steve Matthews, 'Coca-Cola Shelves Dasani Debut in Europe After Recall,' *Bloomberg Business Week,* 24 March, 2004, www.bloomberg.com/apps/news?pid=newsarchive&sid=a9Aisbs7DsFU&refer=top_world_news-redirectoldpage.

12. Divine law or moral code, derived from the Qur'an and the sunnah, as interpreted by classical jurists; some modernists limit Shariah to Qur'an.

13. *Sahih Muslim,* trans. Abdul Hamid Siddiqi (Beirut: Dar Al Arabia, n.d.), book 10: hadith 3798.

14. According to the EPA, the term 'navigable waters', as defined in section 502(7) of the FWPCA (the Federal Water Pollution Control Act, also known as the Clean Water Act), includes interstate waters; intrastate lakes, rivers, and streams that are utilised by interstate travelers for recreational or other pur-

poses; and intrastate lakes, rivers, and streams from which fish or shellfish are taken and sold in interstate commerce.

15. U.S. Environmental Protection Agency, Clean Water Act, www.epa.gov/oecaagct/lcwa.html.

16. *Sahih Muslim,* book 70, hadith 10.

Chapter 11: The Wonderful World of Wudu

1. MyCharity: Water, www.charitywater.org.

2. 'Water: Our Thirsty World', special issue, *National Geographic,* April 2010, 80–95.

3. *Sahih Muslim,* trans. Abdul Hamid Siddiqi (Beirut: Dar Al Arabia, n.d.), book 10: hadith 10.

4. The average person uses 3 to 4 litres of water during ablution. If 1.4 billion Muslims perform ablution five times a day (before each call to prayer), that accounts for over 147 billion litres of water used a week on ablution alone. For more information on water conservation and ablution practices see Ir Noor Azahari Zainal Abidin, 'Operational Aspects of Water Demand Management' Ministry of Energy, Green Technology and Water, Malaysia, www .jba.gov.my/index.php/muat-turun/doc_download/78-operational -aspects-of-water-demand-management.

5. All Dulles Area Muslim Society, *Adams Green Environment Guide* (Washington, DC: Adams Center, 2009). For further information, please see the Adams Center Web site, http://www. adamscenter.org.

6. Al Arabiya News Channel, 'Malaysia Invents Hi-Tech 'Wudu' Machine,' 2 February, 2010, www.alarabiya.net/articles/ 2010/02/02/99094.html#000.

PART IV Food

1. Comment made by Dr. Hal Taussig, Visiting Professor of New Testament, Union Theological Seminary, at the Ninth

Annual Interfaith Iftar Fast Break, 'Diet or Buy It? Faith, Food, and Resource Consumption', 15 September, 2009 (see ch. 3, n. 5).

2. Comments made by Yasir Syeed at the Forty-seventh Annual Islamic Society National Convention, Rosemont, IL, 4 July, 2010.

Chapter 12: Feeding Your Family

1. For information on Halal Advocates of America, see http://halaladvocates.org/wordpress/about.

2. Comments made by Shaykh Abdullah Nana at a presentation titled 'Resetting the Food Systems', Forty-seventh Annual Islamic Society National Convention, Rosemont, IL, 4 July, 2010. Speakers included Shireen Pisheadi, Yusuf Khan, Yasir Syeed, Abdullah Nana, and moderator Qaid Hassan.

3. For more on veganism, see http://vegan.org/frequently-asked-questions/.

4. The following material on Zachary Twist comes from interviews with Zachary by the author on 15 October, 2009, and 27 April, 2010.

5. The material in this section is taken from an interview with Labinsky Roach and Ridwan Falah by the author on 18 November, 2009.

Chapter 13: Urban and Suburban Food Gardens

1. 'First World War Liberty Gardens', http://sidewalksprouts.wordpress.com/history/vg.

2. 'Three Million New York City Residents Living in High Need Neighborhoods Lack Reliable Access to Fresh and Healthy Food', press release, 12 April, 2010, Kirsten Gillibrand, U.S. Senator for New York, http://www.gillibrand.senate.gov/newsroom/press/release/gillibrand-velazquez-quinn-join-white-house-push-to-bring-fresh-food-to-new-yorks-underserved-communities. For more background on urban food deserts, read Sarah Treuhaft

and Allison Karpyn's study 'The Grocery Gap: Who Has Access to Healthy Food and Why It Matters', PolicyLink and the Food Trust, 2010, www.policylink.org/atf/cf/%7B97C6D565-BB43-406D -A6D5-ECA3BBF35AF0%7D/FINALGroceryGap.pdf.

3. 'The Grocery Gap', 18.

4. 'State of the Earth 2010', *National Geographic,* November 2009, 72.

5. The material on Tasleema's urban roof garden is from an interview with Tasleema Jini by the author on 8 November, 2009.

6. For more information on hydroponics, see 'History of Hydroponics', Boswyck Farms, 2010, www.boswyckfarms.org/ history.

Chapter 14: The Farmers' Market

1. Qaid Hassan's story is from an interview with Qaid by the author on 3 October, 2009.

2. For more information on the Nation of Islam, see www.noi.org.

3. Sister Clara Muhammad Schools, http://mohammedschools. org/.

4. For definitions of *dhabihah* and *halal,* see the glossary at the end of the book, and also chapter 15, 'Green Dhabihah'.

5. Qaid started Whole Earth Meats, and I have personally tasted some of their products. If you live in the Chicago area, this should be your go-to source for meat. See http://wholeearthmeats.com.

6. *Sahih Al-Bukhari,* trans. Muhammad Muhsin Khan (Ankara: Islamic University, Al Medina Al Munauwara, n.d.), book 10: hadith 10.

7. Statements on the importation of foods from southern farms to northern African American urban areas are based the author's conversations with local grocery store owners in Bedford-Stuyvesant, Brooklyn, 2009.

8. Qur'an, Surah 14.

Chapter 15: Green Dhabihah

1. *Sunan An-Nasa'i,* trans. Mohammed Mahdi al-Shareef
(Beirut: Dar al-Kutub al-'Ilmiyah, n.d.), book 7: hadith 207.

2. *Sahih Al-Bukhari,* trans. Muhammad Muhsin Khan (Ankara:
Islamic University, Al Medina Al Munauwara, n.d.), book 56:
hadith 689.

3. Richard C. Foltz, *Animals in Islamic Tradition and Muslim
Cultures* (Oxford: One World, 2006), 25.

4. Ibid.

5. Qur'an 16:120–121.

Chapter 16: American Halal—Setting the Stage for the Future

1. 'Pioneering a Just Economy', Social Venture Network Fall
2006 conference, 12–16 October, Tucson, Arizona, www.svn.org/
index.cfm?pageId=1005.

2. These and other remarks by Adnan Durrani at the 2009
American Muslim Consumer Conference are from notes taken by
the author at the conference. For more information on the annual
American Muslim Consumer Conference, see http://american
muslimconsumer.com.

3. The Green Deen practices of the Adams Center, home of the
DC Green Muslims, are discussed in chapters 3, 4, and 11 of this
book.

Conclusion: Following the Call

1. Seyyed Hossein Nasr, *Man and Nature: The Spiritual Crisis in
Modern Man* (Chicago: ABC International Group, Inc., 1997), 5.
Originally published as *Man and Nature: The Spritual Crisis of
Modern Man* (London: Unwin, 1976).

adl Justice.

Allah The Arabic word for God. Allah is the God of Judaism, Christianity, and Islam.

amanah Trust. The covenant we have with God to act as stewards of the Earth.

ayah Three meanings: (1) one of the 6,236 verses of the Qu'ran; (2) one of the signs of God around us—the mountains, the trees, the seas; (3) a miracle.

'Bismillah Allahu Akbar' 'In the name of God, God is Great.' Islamic blessing repeated before slaughtering an animal for food.

caliph According to Sunnis, a successor to the Prophet Muhammad (peace be upon him) as leader of the community.

Deen In Arabic, a religion or a creed, a faith or a belief, a path or a way.

dhabihah Meat hand-slaughtered by a Muslim in an Islamically lawful way, in which animals are sacrificed as humanely as possible and the meat is blessed. *Dhabihah* meat is *halal* and has also been slaughtered with the proper Islamic blessing of 'Bismillah Allahuakbar' ('In the name of God, God is Great').

dhikr An Islamic devotional act.

dua Supplication.

eco-mosque See *Green Mosque*.

Eid Muslim holiday marking the end of Ramadan.

Eid Al-Adha Celebration marking the end of the Hajj.

fatwa Nonbinding legal opinion rendered by a religious scholar.

fitrah Nature, (natural) disposition, constitution, temperament, innate character, instinct; can also mean intuition or insight. As used in this book, the essence of Allah.

five pillars of Islam Faith in One God; five daily prayers; giving charity; fasting during the holy month of Ramadan; making the pilgrimage, or Hajj, to Mecca once in a lifetime.

Green Deen The choice to practise the religion of Islam while affirming the relationship between faith and the environment.

Green Mosque A mosque that follows the six principles of a Green Deen: (1) understanding the Oneness of God and His creation (*tawhid*); (2) seeing signs of God (*ayat*) everywhere; (3) being a steward of the Earth (*khalifah*); (4) honouring the trust we have with God (*amanah*); (5) moving toward justice (*adl*); (6) living in balance with nature (*mizan*).

Green Muslims Muslims who are actively involved in the environmental movement and who are living the six principles of a Green Deen.

hadith Authoritative report of a saying or action of the Prophet Muhammad (peace be upon him).

Hafiz One who has memorised the entire Qur'an.

Hajj The pilgrimage to Mecca that Muslims are required to make once in their lifetime.

halal Permissible; lawful. *Halal* meat is lawful meat—any kind of poultry, beef, goat, and the like that has been slaughtered in a clean and humane way, even if it does not have the proper Islamic blessing of 'Bismillah Allahuakbar' ('In the name of God, God is Great'). Traditionally, animals slaughtered by 'people of the book', meaning Christians and Jews, are *halal* for Muslims to eat.

haram Impermissible.

hijab The traditional head covering for Muslim women.

imam In general, any leader of a Muslim community.

khalifah Steward, vice-regent, or caretaker. As used in this book, a steward of the Earth.

masjid Mosque.

mizan Balance.

mosque All types of buildings dedicated to Islamic worship.

Oneness of creation The belief that everything is connected to God—that we are all part of the same fabric of creation.

'People of the Book' Jews, Christians, and Muslims—those who believe in the One Omnipotent God and whose prophets were sent down with books from that One God to guide the people.

Qur'an The Holy Book revealed to Prophet Muhammad (peace be upon him) in the Arabic language.

Ramadan The ninth month of the Islamic calendar, celebrated as the month the Qu'ran was first revealed to the Prophet Muhammad (peace be upon him). During Ramadan, Muslims abstain from eating, drinking, and physical relations with spouses from sunup to sundown for thirty days.

sadaqa jareyah Ongoing charity that has positive effects even after one's death.

salams Refers to the greeting or blessing 'Al-salamu 'alaykum' ('Peace and Blessings Be upon You') and the reply, 'Wa 'alaykum al-salam' ('And Peace and Blessings Be upon You'). 'Giving salams' means relaying the above blessings or greetings.

Shariah Divine law or moral code, derived from the Qur'an and the sunnah, as interpreted by classical jurists. Some modernists limit Shariah to the Qur'an.

shaykh An honourific term meaning 'elder'. Commonly used to designate a revered wise man or an Islamic scholar.

six principles of a Green Deen (1) Understanding the Oneness of God and His creation (*tawhid*); (2) seeing signs of God (*ayat*) everywhere; (3) being a steward of the Earth (*khalifah*); (4) honouring the trust we have with God (*amanah*); (5) moving toward justice (*adl*); (6) living in balance with nature (*mizan*).

sunnah What the Prophet Muhammad (peace be upon him) did: how he prayed, worshipped, dressed, ate, and spoke; how he was at home, in public, and the like.

surah Chapter. The Qur'an is divided into 114 surahs.

Surah al-Shams The ninety-first surah, or chapter of the Qur'an. In English, 'The Sun'.

tafsir Commentary, or interpretation, of the Qur'an.

tawhid The Oneness of God and His creation.

tayyib Literally, 'good'. *Tayyib* meat comes from animals that were raised properly, fed properly, allowed to graze freely, and allowed to act in the most natural way—the way God intended.

Umrah The 'lesser pilgrimage' to Mecca.

wudu Islamic ritual cleansing before prayer or other important acts of worship. Some people aspire to stay in a state of *wudu* at all times.

zulm Injustice.

General

Council on American-Islamic Relations   www.cair.com
Fiqh Council of North America   www.fiqhcouncil.org
Islam.com   www.islam.com
Islamic Circle of North America   www.icna.org
IslamicFinder.org   www.islamicfinder.com
Islamic Networks Group   www.ing.org
Islamic Relief Worldwide   www.islamic-relief.com
Islamic Society of North America   www.isna.net
Muslim Alliance in North America   www.mana-net.org
Muslim Public Affairs Council   www.mpac.org
Muslim Students Association   www.msanational.org
Ta'leef Collective   www.taleefcollective.org
UMMA Community Clinic   www.ummaclinic.org
Zaytuna College   http://www.zaytunacollege.org/

Building the Green Deen Movement

Ella Baker Center for Human Rights   www.ellabakercenter.org
Ellison for Congress   www.keithellison.org
Future 5000   www.future5000.com

Green Deen: What Islam Teaches About Protecting the Planet,
    www.greendeenbook.com
Green Faith, Interfaith Partners for the Environment
    www.greenfaith.org
Inner-City Muslim Action Network   www.imancentral.org
Interfaith Youth Core   www.ifyc.org
Movement Strategy Center   www.movementstrategy.org
Project South, Institution for the Elimination of Poverty and
    Genocide   www.projectsouth.org
Wellstone Action!   www.wellstone.org

PART I: Waste

Climate Crisis   www.climatecrisis.net
Story of Stuff Project   www.storyofstuff.com

Conservation as Part of a Green Deen

National Wildlife Federation   www.nwf.org
Wildlife Conservation Society   www.wcs.org

Environmental Justice—Peoples' Environmentalism

Environmental Health Coalition   www.environmentalhealth.org
Environmental Justice Advocates of Minnesota   www.ejamn.org
Generational Alliance   http://generationalalliance.org
United Puerto Rican Organization of Sunset Park
    www.uprose.org
WE ACT for Environmental Justice   www.weact.org

Environmental Regulation and Protection

Natural Resources Defense Council   www.nrdc.org
Sierra Club   www.sierraclub.org
U.S. Environmental Protection Agency   www.epa.gov

Green Muslims and Green Mosques

Adams Center   www.adamscenter.org
Green Deen   http://greendeen.wordpress.com
Green Muslims in the District   http://green-muslims.org/
Green Zabiha   www.greenzabiha.com
Interfaith Center of New York   www.interfaithcenter.org
Islamic Foundation for Ecology and Environmental Sciences
    http://ifees.org.uk
Islamic Society of Greater Houston   www.isgh.org
Liberal Arts Forum   http://liberalartsforum.com
Lighthouse Mosque   www.lighthousemosque.org
Ta'Leef Collective   www.taleefcollective.org

PART II: Watts

Solar One   http://solar1.org
U.S. Department of Energy   www.energy.gov

Energy from Heaven

Bright Power   www.brightpower.biz
IBM Smart Grid   www.ibm.com/smarterplanet/us/en/smart_grid/
    ideas
Indigenous Environmental Network   www.ienearth.org
Native Harvest   http://nativeharvest.com
Solar Center   www.thesolarcenter.com

Energy from Hell

Coal River Wind   http://www.crmw.net/

Green Jobs

Apollo Alliance   http://apolloalliance.org
Center on Wisconsin Strategy (COWS)   www.cows.org

Emerald Cities Collaborative   www.emeraldcities.org
Green for All   www.greenforall.org

PART III: Water

Charity: Water   www.charitywater.org
FLOW: For Love of Water   www.flowthefilm.com
Food and Water Watch   www.foodandwaterwatch.org
Global Water   www.globalwater.org
Immerse Global   www.immerseglobal.com
Ohio Valley Environmental Coalition   www.ohvec.org
Water.org   www.water.org

PART IV: Food

American Halal Co, Inc.   http://www.saffronroadfood.com/
Bryant Terry   www.bryant-terry.com
Crescent Foods   www.crescenthalal.com
Food, Inc.   http://www.takepart.com/foodinc
Green Zabiha   www.greenzabiha.com
Jamie Oliver   www.jamieoliver.com
Park Slope Food Coop   http://foodcoop.com
People's Grocery   www.peoplesgrocery.org
Slow Food International   www.slowfood.com
Stonyfield Farm   www.stonyfield.com
Zabihah   www.zabihah.com

Acknowledgments

All thanks and praise due to Almighty God. Peace and blessings to Prophets Muhammad, Adam, Ibrahim, Ismail, Isaac, Solomon, Moses, Salih, and Jesus—peace be with them all. Blessings to Imam Siraj Wahhaj from Masjid At-Taqwa in Brooklyn, Shaykh Mokhtar Maghraoui from New York State's Capital District, Imam Zaid Shakir of the Zaytuna Institute in California, and Sidi Usama Canon of the Ta'Leef Collective in northern California—may Allah forgive them of their sins and grant them and their families and associates all a high station in paradise.

Blessings to my grandparents, and to all my ancestors who suffered the horrors of the slave trade travelling from Africa, and to my North American First Nation forebearers who endured the destruction of their traditional way of life. We walk in the paths they forged, honouring the prayers they made in times of great adversity.

Many thanks go to my mother and father for their patience with me and my path. They surrounded us with more books than we could ever count. And I thank Auntie Amina for her consistent critical thinking. I am grateful to my brother

Karim for reviewing almost every document I have ever completed; to my sister Jehan for keeping me honest; to my youngest sister Tauhirah for imploring me to get to studying my Islam and stop wasting my time; to my sister Adilah for being full of unconditional love; and to my big little brother Ali for being independent minded and always selfless when it comes to family—he's the true ninja.

Green Deen would not have been possible without the influence of a great many people. May Allah give all of the following the best of this life and of the next and save them from the worst of this life and the trials of the next: The foresight of Sophia Kizilbash, Suad Abdul-Khabeer, and Kauthar Umar brought together the Muslim Alliance in North America panel that helped provide the framework for this book. Mohamad Chakaki and Faraz Khan are two men who are far more qualified to write and speak on this topic than I. From Washington, DC, particularly Sanjana Ahmad, Zaynab Aden, and Sarah Jawaid provided key insights in the development of this book. Huge blessings to Karen Monahan, who helped secure the connection with Congressman Ellison, who wrote the foreword. Of course, *Green Deen* would not have been possible had it not been for Deanna Zandt (fellow upstate New Yorker and author of *Share This!*) and breakfast at Dizzy's.

The following people all contributed in some way to the development of *Green Deen:* Musa, Ahlam, and Yasir Syeed; Dr. L'Heaureux Lewis; Amir Al-Islam; Sister Aisha Al-Adiwiyya; Rami Nashashibi; Asad Jafri; Debbie Almontaser; Nimco Ahmed; Idris Braithwaite and Ismail Ocasio; Abu's Bakery; Abdul Qadir; Van Jones; Ashel; JBless; Omar Mullick; Samiha Rahman; Professors Sonia Jarvis, Ed Sermier, Rosa

Marie Pegueros, Al Killilea, Lynn Pasquerella, and Cynthia Hamilton.

Much appreciation to Yusef Ramelize, Jungwon and Soyoung Kim, Taj James, Wajiha Akhtar and Awais Khaleel, Zaid Mohiuddin, Tanjila Islam, Najma Nazyat, Terry Marshall, Nisrin Elamin, May Alhassen, Anas Canon, Mahea and Alea, Kizzy Charles-Guzman, Bracken Hendricks, Marianne Manilov, Jodie Tonita, Ferentz Lafargue, CAIR-NY, the Green For All Fellows, and the 2008 National Urban Fellows.

My editor at Berrett-Koehler in San Francisco was Johanna Vondeling—there are no words that can describe her patience, her courage, her ease and calm, and her abilities. I am blessed to have worked with her on this project. Many thanks also to managing editor Jeevan Sivasubramaniam and the rest of the Berrett-Koehler family. The mechanics of 'finishing' a book are astounding. To that production team I owe a great deal of gratitude.

David Peattie of BookMatters, Berkeley, California, shepherded the book through the final detailed steps of copyediting, typesetting, proofreading, and indexing. I am most grateful to him and to my infinitely capable copyeditor Mary Anne Stewart, eagle-eyed proofreader Kirsten Janene-Nelson, and meticulous indexer Gerald Van Ravenswaay.

Recognising that only Allah makes a pair, I finally, but most importantly, thank my wife, Fatima Ashraf, who taught me the meaning of the word loyalty.

Index

About the Author

For the past ten years, Ibrahim Abdul-Matin has been a passionate voice for transforming our pollution-based way of life to one that prioritises our planet and its people. Early on, Ibrahim discovered that working with young people, people of faith, and environmental advocates allowed him the best opportunity to meld his passions with his skills to develop a unique movement, the Green Deen movement, that eventually anyone could be a part of.

Born in 1977 and raised Muslim, Ibrahim developed a deep sense of spirituality early on. However, as a child of converts to Islam, he faced challenges while developing his own religious identity. The diversity of the Muslim American community included a variety of cultures and traditions that he tried and debated before settling on a personal practice that gave centrality to serving God, people, and planet. Simultaneously, he was strengthening his relationship to the natural world as he learned about his ancestors and their connection to the land as farmers and landowners in upstate New York, southern Virginia, and Nebraska.

As a child, Ibrahim moved from Brooklyn to small-town Sidney, New York, and then later as a teenager to the industrial city of Troy, New York. During these years, he was exposed to the cultural arts movement in the black community, the traditional American small-town experience, and the challenges of the crime and violence of the crack era. He navigated these challenges by becoming a voracious reader and an accomplished athlete. Eventually athletics afforded him a full scholarship to the University of Rhode Island, where he excelled as a student, a political organiser, and a spoken-word poet. In college he came to understand the need for civic action around sustainability to protect the planet. He graduated in 1999 wanting to do two things: publish a book and change the world.

Ibrahim began his 'change the world' agenda working with Corporate Accountability International in Boston on their boycott of Kraft Foods, then owned by Philip Morris. It was also in Boston that he cofounded Urban Griots, a poetry-reading collective in the Lucy Parsons Center, where he and other young organisers conducted political education sessions and shared their spoken words and poetry. He also soon started working with Outward Bound on Thompson Island in Boston Harbor, where he led programmes for at-risk youth that emphasised personal growth through experience and challenge in the wilderness.

Upon returning to New York, Ibrahim helped to create a national database of youth organisers. The *Future 500* was published in 2002, and the print edition was later expanded online and re-released as the *Future 5000*. He then took the position of director of youth programmes at the Prospect Park Alliance. There Ibrahim trained middle and high school students to understand how their actions can hurt, or help, the planet. In this role, he also helped to establish the Brooklyn Academy of Science and the Environment, which today is a successful high school of almost five hundred students dedicated to academic excellence with an environmental focus.

In 2004, Ibrahim left Prospect Park for California to work for the Movement Strategy Center, a progressive think tank focussing on building social justice movements. Here, he learned the ABCs of movement building, networking, fundraising, and organising. On the West Coast, Ibrahim also had the unique opportunity to study Arabic at the premiere Zaytuna College. His involvement with Zaytuna and Bay Area mosques, including Masjid al-Iman and the Lighthouse Mosque, were instrumental in strengthening his Green Dean.

Back in New York, Ibrahim was accepted into the prestigious National Urban Fellows programme and received a master's degree in public administration from Baruch College. His area of expertise—environmental policy—landed him a fellowship with Green For All, an organisation dedicated to improving America through a clean-energy economy. Ibrahim was instrumental in organising Green For All's National Day of Action calling for 'Green Jobs Now'. On that day, more than fifty thousand Americans from over seven hundred communities voiced their support of a green economy with green jobs.

While writing *Green Deen* and being based in New York City, Ibrahim worked as a consultant for several organisations, including Green City Force and the Inner-City Muslim Action Network (IMAN). At each of these organisations, he emphasised the importance of youth, faith, and the environment and how together they are the ingredients for a solid social justice movement.

Ibrahim has become an interfaith leader in his own right. His writings on faith and the environment have been featured in *Common Ground, ColorLines, WireTap, Left Turn,* and *Elan* magazines, and he is the brains behind the popular blog 'Brooklyn Bedouin'. He is a widely requested speaker nationwide by Muslim organizations, interfaith groups, universities, and environmental advocates. Ibrahim is also teaching faith leaders about Islam and the environment and has been a featured speaker for the Yale University Chaplain's Office and the 'Farm the Land, Grow the Spirit' interfaith internship in Stony Point, New York.

Today, Ibrahim is using all of his expertise in youth development, movement building, environmental knowledge, and deep spiritual roots in his work as a policy adviser in Mayor Michael Bloomberg's office, focussing on issues of long-term planning and sustainability. Ibrahim lives in Brooklyn Heights with his wife and their small urban garden of herbs and onions.